Lessons from the Bored Room

How to Avoid Meeting Monotony,
Be a Better Speaker,
and Make Your Communication Sing

© 2012 by AccuConference

Maranda Gibson

David Byrd

George Page

ISBN: 1466282614

ISBN-13: 9781466282612

Contents

Foreword
Written by: Ken Molay
President, Webinar Success

"The burden of communications rests on the communicator." I honestly can't remember when or where I first heard that quote. Probably from my father, who worked in public relations and advertising his entire career and knew a thing or two about the power of effective communications. The strength and simplicity of the message has stayed with me over decades of professional and personal interactions. If you have something to say, it's your responsibility to have it be heard, understood, and appreciated by your audience.

It's true when you speak one-to-one with a peer. It's true when you present an idea in a team setting. It's true when you stand in front of a room giving a speech. And it's true when you present to a remote audience via the telephone or computer.

Your goal may be educational. It may be related to sales and marketing. Perhaps your objective is to influence your audience's perception of you or your business offerings. You might be sharing information to advance a project. No matter the situation, you own the task of getting people to listen, assimilate your points, and retain the information for application in their personal or work lives.

When I think back over my career and personal hobbies, I am struck by how important effective communication techniques have been. You may not have taken the same path I did or shared the same specific examples, but I'll bet you can come up with your own comparable experiences:

- Working in college study groups to share information and present it clearly and persuasively to the teacher
- Leading work projects and taking on coordination and management of team meetings
- Working trade show booths, interacting with visitors and concisely conveying key persuasive points
- Giving talks at conferences and industry gatherings
- Holding telephone conferences with press and analysts to influence their views of our company and offerings
- Presenting budgets, department plans, and requests for approval to senior management

The effectiveness of my communications in each of these scenarios fundamentally affected my success and opportunities to advance. The ability to communicate important concepts clearly, effectively, and persuasively within a given setting alters how others perceive you. You may have heard the old chestnut that "it is better to keep your mouth closed and let people think you are a fool than to open it and remove all doubt." But there is another side to that coin.

Former US president Ronald Reagan is frequently referenced as "The Great Communicator." Agree or disagree with his politics and actions while in office, his communication skills remain legendary to this day. He called on his previous acting experience, his radio broadcasting background, and his years as a corporate spokesman to shape a speaking style that was comfortable and homespun, conversational, and personal; yet at the same time confident, insistent, and specific about desired actions and outcomes. Reagan could work a room, steer a telephone meeting towards his desired objectives, or give a galvanizing speech heard by unseen millions.

I often work with business presenters who press me for a magical tactic "to make people pay attention." I have bad news for you... You can't *make* people pay attention. That went out with sour-faced teachers slamming rulers onto the knuckles of daydreaming students. In a world of telephone and web presentations, you're going to need an awfully long ruler.

Audiences pay attention when presented with content that is interesting, relevant, and useful to *them*, not just to you as the speaker. They pay attention when they feel engaged, involved, and respected. They pay attention when your vocal techniques, presentation style, and audience interaction pull them in and continually reengage them. And they pay attention when the accompanying communications technology is used competently and unobtrusively to support the presentation.

The book you are about to launch into covers a wide range of communication scenarios, tips, and technologies. It starts with a deceptively simple meeting and presentation technology -- the telephone. What device is more commonplace and familiar than the good old phone? And yet... And yet... Can any of us say that we have never been on a conference call that seemed tedious, poorly thought out, and ineffective in accomplishing its goal? How can something as simple as an audio conference produce such feelings of exasperation? Starting from first principles might not be such a bad idea to see if we can make audio conferences something to be anticipated rather than dreaded.

As you continue reading, you will pick up tips on speaking techniques, meeting organization and administration, dealing with presentation anxiety, and the similarities and differences between speaking to people in the same room and speaking to people who may be thousands of miles distant. You will work up to the latest approaches in remote collaboration... web conferences, webinars, and webcasts. You will learn ways to affect attendance and interest in your topic before the meeting.

I have a selfish reason for hoping you will take the offered tips to heart and look for ways to improve your meetings and presentations. I just might be in your audience. And I'd sure appreciate the consideration you show in working to make the experience more enjoyable and valuable for me. I won't even mind that it provides more value back to you and your company as well. On behalf of all your meeting participants everywhere, thank you for caring!

Ken Molay is the President and founder of Webinar Success, a consulting company focusing on providing skills for the preparation and delivery of successful webinars in a variety of markets. Webinar Success provides one on one instruction and training for the busy professional.

Introduction
By Chilton Tippin

AccuConference started as a simple calling card business. We provided calling cards to traveling employees so they could stay in contact with their families while on the road. But soon we began to notice a trend in the communications industry: cell phones were getting cheaper and more widely available. As this occurred, calling cards would become obsolete.

By 2001 we realized we needed to adapt or die. The question was "how?" If employees would soon be making calls on mobile phones, what would be the next best thing to offer? That's when we realized that as companies spread out they would need more diverse forms of communication to simultaneously hold them together. Our solution: multi-line conferences, ranging in size from two to 1,000 participants.

As time progressed and our platform got more customized and advanced, we began to gather a good deal of knowledge on the topic of communication itself. How does one give a strong presentation? What are the best practices when conducting a conference call? Our clients would ask questions such as these and we'd do our best to answer them. We didn't always know the answer, but through trial and error we grew to understand communications more and more. After all, when you've made yourself a medium of communication for thousands of individuals, it would be hard not to learn a thing or two about the subject along the way.

In time, we began passing that advice along in the form of a blog on our website. We used our blog to share the things we learned about conferencing, meetings, public relations, and corporate communications. This book is a distillation of those blog posts. We've taken our favorite pieces, tweaked them, organized them into sections, and published them here.

The first part of the book deals with the nuts and bolts of conference calling. It will walk you through practical considerations, like preparing your team for a conference call and deciding whether a phone-based call would be optimal for your given situation. It will impart helpful tips for increasing attendance on calls and making invitations, and even warn against some of the common mistakes that moderators make (assuming the line is muted).

From that point we begin to discuss important presentation techniques. Based on the notion that any conference call is simply a presentation over the phone, these tips will give you guidance on how to speak with confidence and drive your message home. In addition, you will get advice on creating web-based PowerPoint presentations and running polls and chats, all features that can help supplement any conference call.

Toward the end, you will find details about webinars: how they can help your business, whether you should charge for them, how to market for them, and when to schedule.

With the advice in this book, you should be more than prepared for anything conferencing. We've interspersed practical advice with rich anecdotes and tips to try to make it both entertaining and useful. Conferencing is a tool that can truly open a world of possibilities for your organization, and this book will give you a good idea of how to unlock that potential.

Chilton Tippin joined AccuConference in 2010. He contributes to the AccuConference blog, all.pro blog, and SignalNews. com, our technology news site.

About the Authors

Maranda Gibson joined AccuConference in 2009 and began writing for the AccuConference blog. She is the head writer at AccuConference as well as the face behind the company's social media profiles on Twitter and Facebook.

David Byrd is the VP of Operations at AccuConference and gives a unique perspective to the readers of our blog by offering his take on business changes, growth, and new technologies.

George Page is a contributor to the AccuConference blog and has been a huge part of growing the AccuConference blog over the previous six years. His work can also been seen in the *Ruins Terra* and *Mirror Shards* anthologies.

Part One: Getting the Most out of Your Conference Calls

-- *To Teleconference, or Not to Teleconference, That Is the Question!*

There's a lot of talk these days about how people should do more conference calling to save money. We all know, however, that there are some things you just can't do or information you can't get in a conference call. Below are some questions to consider when deciding whether a traditional meeting, a conference call, or a videoconference is the best option for your meeting.

Consider what you hope to achieve in the meeting. Maybe everything can be accomplished by email. Or does the meeting goal depend on observing body language or on high levels of personal interaction, trust, and relationship building?

How many people will be involved? If you have 12 people involved, each person only has, on average, 5 minutes to speak. Does that justify the expense of a face-to-face?

How dependent is the content on visual images that you need to walk your participants through? Will it hurt if they can't see what's going on?

If your group is spread out geographically, what will be the effect of different time zones on people's ability to be there and alert? This is an increasingly important consideration as more businesses go global.

Once you know the answers to these questions, you can determine whether you need just a plain vanilla teleconference, a videoconference, or a real face-to-face meeting.

-- Conference Call Checklist

So you want to have a conference call? No problem; you can start one in minutes. The first thing is to ask the following questions: when, who, what, and where.

Once you've worked out when to have the call (see "What's the Best Time and Day to Have a Conference Call" later in this book), decide who's going to be there. Also, will you have a guest speaker, or will you host the meeting and do the talking? Next, decide how long the meeting needs to run. Once that's settled, write out what the meeting is going to be about and create an agenda, making sure to estimate how long each point will take. It's always good to give yourself 5-10 minutes of margin. And don't forget to budget time for questions.

Now that you have all that planned, it's time to do some inviting. Your email invitations should include: what the meeting is about; the call-in number and participant code; when the meeting is and for how long; an abbreviated version of the agenda.

Finally, where will you be? The beauty of conference calling is that you can do it from pretty much anywhere. Your only constraints are to conduct the call from a quiet place where you won't be interrupted and, for best sound quality, to use a landline.

One last suggestion: Use a headset. It's much more comfortable than cradling the phone in your neck.

-- Planning for the Call

Let's say you need a meeting of the minds with people in a faraway branch of your company. You may need to coordinate with the members there to go over the agenda and goals of the meeting beforehand. You will likely be able to get all this figured out through phone calls and emails, but it might be better to have a quick chat via teleconference.

It's a cliché, but there often needs to be a meeting before the meeting. Since you have to get everything set for the teleconference anyway, why not meet with your fellow planners right beforehand? You can discuss logistics immediately before the call, and early arrivers won't be able to hear a thing because their lines will still be muted. Perform a sound check, calm jitters, do all you need to do right before the main conference starts. You have the technology already in hand, so why not set aside a little extra time to make sure things go smoothly?

-- *Practice Makes Perfect*

If you're the main speaker for a conference call or web conference, be sure to practice before the day of the call or event. You can assure yourself that your audience will get the full impact of your message by taking the time to be prepared. What you really shouldn't do is try to conduct a conference call in an "off-the-cuff" fashion. Prepare your notes ahead of time. Think about the main topic, what you want to say, and the length of the call. Remember that people in other places will be hearing, but not seeing, you. They will likely be taking notes themselves, so you have to present your theme in a digestible fashion.

Once you have your notes in good shape, it's time to practice saying them aloud. You can't replicate what will happen during the call, but you can be familiar with what you want to say. Record yourself using your notes to give the presentation and then play it back to get an idea of how you might sound. Ask your spouse or a friend to listen as you give a practice presentation. This person can then ask a few clarifying questions and give you feedback.

-- *What's the Best Time and Day to Have a Conference Call?*

The best day and time for a conference call depends mostly on your business and the time zone you're calling, but here are a few commonsense guidelines to help you choose:

Stay away from Monday morning. Monday morning is usually reserved for putting out fires from the weekend or for tasking staff members for the week. If you need to phone on Monday, do it after 2:00 P.M., when most of the heavy workload is out of the way.

Avoid Friday afternoon, too. Some people will leave early on Friday or are working a compressed week schedule and are off every other Friday. If you phone on Friday, do it in the morning around 10:00, after the morning rush but not so late as to interfere with the plans of the day.

Tuesday, Wednesday, and Thursday may be best for your needs. If the conference call is about tasking, Tuesday will be best so as to allow team members time to complete tasks for the week. If the topic is accountability, Thursday may be better, as you will have more data from the week to review. Wednesday is great for training, communications, reviews, and new directions or brainstorming sessions. People are in the swing of things on Wednesday and feeling more relaxed. They still have time to take on a new project before the end of the workweek. Wednesday mornings seem to work better than afternoons.

Whichever day you choose, understand that the best day for you is most likely an individual choice driven by the needs of your business and your personal schedule. Perhaps at the end of your next conference call, you can decide as a group the best day for the following call. You may find that the middle of the week will simply be the best for your team too.

-- Two Tips for Better Preparation

The number one rule of conference calling is to not wait until the last moment. If you get an invitation for a conference, put it on your calendar and make sure you're aware of it. For those hosting a conference call, be sure you've been upfront about the subject of the call. If you're on a team meeting for a new project, make sure the invitees know this is what the call is about. Never assume that people will know. You need to have the right people come prepared with the right information to make it work.

If you're participating in a conference, make sure you read the details of the invitation and think, "How does this apply to me?" There's a reason you've been invited. If you're a member of a project team, for instance, what's your role? What information do you have that can make the call a success? If the call is a meeting of a spread-out department, what new information do you need to pass on to the rest of the team?

-- How to Prepare Your Team for a Conference Call

As a manager, you can do a lot to get your team ready for a conference call. Use these tips to ensure everyone is ready to be at their best:

Confirm the day, time, and length of the call at least three times. Send out reminders including this information to your team three times before the meeting. Send it first for their calendars and schedules, then again about a week before (of course, this doesn't work if the call is every week), and then once more the day before. Some folks even send a reminder the morning of the call.

Send out the outline or agenda a few days before the meeting. This way, attendees have time to look it over, formulate ideas and thoughts, and prepare effectively. Distributing notes just before a call defeats the purpose of the conference. Also, ask attendees to add their own items. That way, everyone has a chance to help plan the call, and the most pressing issues are all included. Of course, if you do not intend to accomplish a large task during your call, you meet many times a week, or the issues are not complex, it may not be necessary to send out the outline very far in advance. The minimum, though, is four hours before the call.

Use the Five-Minute Rule. The majority of meetings have late arrivers, with most attendees arriving within five minutes after the start time. Go ahead and start on time, but don't give out the "meat" of your presentation until five minutes in. This way, more people will hear the important points of your meeting.

Be open for questions. No matter how much of an effort you make to get the handouts and agenda to attendees beforehand, be understanding if some folks are still a little lost. It happens. Life is stressful. Be courteous and helpful, offer to send them the handouts or agenda again, and try to honestly answer questions as the call progresses.

It's really all about attitude when preparing for a conference. The more easygoing you are, the better things will go. Above all, remember that conferences are made up of human beings capable of error, and that the best-laid plans can always go awry. If you're prepared and have prepared your attendees, the worst thing that can happen is that the power goes out (and it will), the phone line picks up static (it might), and no one shows up (just reschedule). No matter what happens, it helps to be prepared.

-- Planning For Unforeseen Circumstances

In 2011, the city of Arlington, Texas played host to the Super Bowl and there were a myriad of events that were in town. It was a week of events, parties, concerts, and it was also a week of record-breaking winter weather.

We get snow and ice in this area, but it usually only sticks around for a day, with the sun coming out and temperatures rebounding quickly. Four days of below freezing temperatures froze the city and surrounding areas. This caused charity events and celebrity appearances to be cancelled and made it difficult for the NFL teams to get to practice. When the sun finally came out over the weekend, the hibernating citizens ventured out to attend some events. A friend and I made our way to see our favorite band put on a free concert, but we found ourselves waiting in line and eventually turned away from an event that had been improperly scheduled. Now, we can never anticipate something like the ice and snow that fell across our area, but we can try to plan for the unforeseen circumstances. Here are some things we can learn from living in the middle of the unexpected winter blast.

Plan for more attendees than you need. The concert

we attempted to attend was scheduled after a celebrity football game and when more people showed up than expected, the fire marshal had to close the doors. Only those who had an RSVP or an invitation were able to get in (despite the fact that there were people steadily leaving the first event). When planning a conference call event, speak with your conference call provider and find out how many people you can have before needing a reservation. Reserve additional lines over what you expect so that if additional people wish to attend you don't have to turn them away.

Advertise one start time. The event I tried to attend was advertised on the band's site as beginning at 2:30 PM. Those of us that showed up at 1:30 PM were an hour early for that event, but were still turned away because the first event was full. If you're going to have multiple presenters or speakers, send out one start time for the event as a whole, and then send out a detailed agenda about the events going on throughout the day.

Communicate earliest start times. Part of the problem was that the two events advertised different starting times. If the band advertised the first event start time, many of their fans would have been sure to be there at that time. On your conference invitations, let participants know what time they can start dialing in or if space is limited. That way the people who really want to join your conference will be sure they get there early enough to have a seat.

In the end, I listened to the concert on TV later that night and realized that even though some things are seen as "once-in-a-lifetime" events — like the biggest football game of the year or a monumental winter storm, we can't see into the future to know everything that might be coming. We can only plan for the unexpected and give everyone a lot of information upfront so that there are no surprises.

What is your contingency plan in the event of a last minute change?

-- Three Ways to Set Tone with Invitations

As the dutiful and wonderful daughter I am, I recently went to my mother's house to clean it while she was out of town. While there, I stumbled across these beautiful wax stamps I had used to seal my wedding invitations. It made me think about how, when it's something we're excited about, we put a lot of time and effort into sending an invitation. But when it's something business-related, we forget that any invitation is going to affect the tone of the event. Below are three ways you can set the right tone with your conference call invitations.

1. FlashCan evites.[1] These are cute and fun. The site lets you create your own invitation using artist-donated Flash material. I played around for a few minutes, and while the resulting invitations are a little on the campy side, it's a great way to invite co-workers or close business partners to an informal conference. The humorous tone of the invitation will let participants know they're joining a conference call among friends.

2. Press release and registration page. To set a more-formal tone, publish a press release and include a

registration link. The press release goes out online or is sent to individual agencies. The tone created is going to be more serious, and it may not be appropriate if you're hosting a training update or something with your co-workers.

3. Handwritten invitations. Yes, in this crazy technical world where everything can be sent out via email, we should never discount the handwritten invitation. It tells invitees that their participation in the event is valued.

No matter what you're inviting someone to, it's always important to consider the tone you're setting. Since a conference call can be considered a business annoyance, sending out creative invitations is one way to make your next call less of a bore and more of an event, without a dress code.

1 http://www.flashcan.com

-- Tricked by Time Zones

You're not the only one to have been tricked by time zones. We receive multiple calls every day from people who have either been told the wrong time or were confused themselves. It's understandable, considering that there are 9 time zones that span the United States and its territories (not to mention the rest of the world and the other 15 time zones).

Use the address at the end of this article to access a chart of the most-popular time zones for conference calls. Then print a copy for future reference. Each color grid represents an hour. Note that Arizona (AZ) and Indiana (IN) alternate time zones depending on the time of year.

If you don't think you need a time zone chart, here's a test: If you made a call on the Fourth of July from Arizona at 2:00 P.M., what time would it be in New York? Did you need to check the chart to find the answer? If so, you should print it for future reference (The answer is 5:00 P.M.).

The next time you're planning a multi-time zone conference call, send an email to all participants, reminding them of the time difference. Include the correct meeting time for each time zone. And if you host weekly meetings, be sure to plan them on the same day at the same time to prevent confusion.

1 http://www.time.gov/

-- How to Get More People to Attend Your Conference Call

It can be difficult to achieve high attendance numbers at your conference call events, and trying so hard for those high numbers can leave you feeling frustrated. Are you bummed by the low attendance at your last one or two or ten? Read on.

Make sure the call is well publicized. Display information about the conference on your website, blog, Facebook, Twitter, LinkedIn, and below your email signature. Include the correct date and time as well as a descriptive subject. A clear subject will attract more people.

Use discretion when choosing whom to invite. Don't invite every person you know for the sake of attendance numbers. Send invitations to those who you think would be most interested in the topic.

Use incentives to attract listeners. Offer discounts on your services or future conferences to participants who attend.

Send reminders. People may register for the conference in advance and simply forget to dial in. Send registrants an email reminder a few days before the event, and then again one hour before the call begins.

Make your conferences interactive. PowerPoints, documents, polls, chat messaging, and Q&A are all ways to keep your attendants engaged in the call. If the conference is enjoyable and interesting, there is a greater chance your participants will register for one of your future events.

-- Increase Attendance on Conference Calls

There was a sharp increase of teleconference use in 2010, with companies and individuals embracing conference call providers to drive fresh business and clients to their products and services. For those of you who wish to increase attendance on your conference calls, here are a couple of tips from one of our event planners.

Schedule conference times in the time zone best suited for the highest number of people. Chances are a lot of the people you're inviting will be scattered throughout the country, so find the time zone with the highest concentration of folks, and set a time most convenient for them. If 90% of your invites are going out to those on the West Coast, you won't get a high turnout if the call is at 8AM Eastern.

Schedule the teleconference before lunch time. Now that you've squared away the time zone, you need to decide what the best start time will be. We've found that the best time to host a call is between 10 and 11AM, respective to the selected time zone.

Plan ahead and send reminders. The longer you wait to send out invitations, the more likely it will be that people will make other plans. Sending out invitations at least two weeks in advance makes it more likely that people will have the time to attend your conference call. Send them a reminder the morning of the conference in case they have forgotten.

Don't invite everyone. If you want to get the best turn out for your conference, use discretion when choosing who to invite. Send your invitations to the people you think would be the most interested in the conference. For example, if you're trying to sell office supplies, you wouldn't invite the CEO of an office supply chain to your conference.

Make your conference calls interactive. Create Power-Point presentations and share them with your participants. A little visual stimulation can go a long way.

When it comes down to increasing attendees on a webinar or teleconference, there is no perfect formula for getting people to show up and be active on your conferences.

-- *Attracting the Conference Call "No-Shows"*

You completed a successful conference call. Feedback from attendees was very positive. Some perhaps even said it was the best conference call they ever attended. Congratulations! Now pull out that list of those who signed up but did not attend.

Send the no-shows an email containing a link to your archived event. Let them know they have another opportunity to listen to the insightful conference at their convenience. Briefly remind them why doing so is an excellent use of their time. Entice them by quoting a few of the attendees who gave enthusiastic reviews.

In the no-show email, offer people a free trial of your services. If you had requested and received information about their product preferences in the registration form, offer them a tempting product discount. Free offers are also typically welcomed by way of a phone call.

For those who actually attended the call, use an online survey to gather comments after the conference. Their comments can help you create an even better presentation. An online survey will also make them active participants and less likely to "click you off." Remember to place a "contact me" box in the after-the-event email survey. With appealing emails, the no-shows might be clicking the "contact me" box after your next conference call.

-- *Getting the Word Out about Your Teleconferences*

To publicize a series of teleconferences, you have to get creative. Notice we said publicize, not advertise. Of course you can take out ads in trade publications and newspapers, but if your budget is limited, you may want to save those funds for another venture.

Instead of taking out ads, write letters to the editor when you see an article about a topic your teleconference will address. Of course you have to mention the teleconferences in the letter. But don't make it like a commercial. Make sure you concentrate on relevant commentary about the topic at hand, and mention the teleconferences are just one of the ways your organization keeps the public informed.

Make sure you talk about upcoming teleconferences every chance you get. When you meet people at conferences, happy hours, and networking events, don't forget to tell them about what your organization is doing. This seems so simple, but you'd be surprised at just how often we all forget that word of mouth is the best way to promote. Even if you meet people and think they aren't in your industry, tell them about the teleconference anyway. They may know others who'd be interested.

-- Put Your Email Signature to Work Promoting Your Next Conference Call

How often have you received an email in which there was no signature other than the person's name and email address at the bottom? We all get these types of emails, but why not put your email signature to work getting more attendees at your next teleconference?

Think of the space assigned to your email signature as free ad space. Make sure you have not only your name, but also your contact information, as well as a link to your website and a link to the page that tells readers about your upcoming teleconference. Below is just one example that you may want to consider when setting up your own signature:

Janie Smith

President, Image Coaching for Experts

Voice: 1-800-555-1212

Fax: 404-555-1212

Visit us on the Web at http://www.yoursitehere.com

Sign up for our free teleconference on February 15th at 1:00 PST today!

Although these hyperlinks just go to our own website in this example, if you link to an informational page and signup form for your teleconference, you gain the instant opportunity to get more attendees.

When it comes to email, simpler is better, but make sure to use this free real estate to promote your services.

-- How to Conduct Your First Conference Call: A Quick Overview

A conference call can actually be fun. It's a great way to feel connected on a project, inspire a group of people, or feel as if you're in the same room and not a long way away. If you've only attended a conference call and never hosted or presented on a call before, we've collected our best tips to help make your first call a success.

Make sure everyone has the correct time, date, dial-in number, and participant code. The dial-in number is the number participants dial to connect to the conference channel, and the code allows them to enter the private conference call. Expect to have to provide these again to those who may lose or forget the information or panic before they arrive to the call (usually those who are new to attending conference calls). Distribute agenda or presentation printouts before the call. Some presenters prefer not to hand out an agenda before a call, but it's much easier to track the presentation when you have something to look at. Those who don't hand out an agenda beforehand risk getting a lot of questions about whether there will be printouts.

Prepare yourself with backup notes and reminders to speak clearly, calmly, and slowly. The faster you go through your material, the more confusion and questions there will be. Plus, as you force yourself to speak slowly, you'll calm yourself automatically.

Don't be too hard on yourself when you make a mistake. You might stumble over words or mispronounce a name, but everyone makes mistakes. When you do, just keep going, or chuckle a bit if that helps smooth it over. Be gracious if someone points out your mistake, and say thanks. People will remember that more than the mistake.

End on time; don't keep people more than 10 extra minutes if you do go long. If you state your call will be an hour, stick to that time. Nothing is worse than sitting for another 20 minutes waiting for the presenter to wrap it up. People will drop off the call if you go too long.

It's as simple as delivering a clear message, taking questions, and ending the call. The more conference calls you lead, the easier it will become.

-- Use Different Speech Approaches to Get Conference Call Results

In a conference call, your words and how you use them affect how both you and your message are perceived. Basically, people take one of two approaches: the I-centered, in which you exert control over the conversation from the start, or the group-centered, which encourages participation from the entire group. The approach you use depends on your goal.

Let's take a look at some of the statements you might use in each approach. I-centered: "My experience indicates that the plan is workable/impractical." "I agree/disagree with that idea." "I would argue that ..." "I'm in favor of/opposed to ..." "I'd like to review the (budget, timeline, analysis, etc.)." "I have several thoughts on how we can solve this problem." Group-centered: "Is there more to this issue?" "Interesting ... go on." "What else do we need to discuss?" "What do you recommend?" "I wonder if we should consider the (budget, timeline, analysis, etc.)."

In the group-centered approach, it's also good sometimes to say nothing. Silence often elicits expansion on a statement or provides a void that encourages another person to speak.

You may find it beneficial to use different approaches at different points in the call. You might begin with an I-centered statement that defines the objective and parameters of the call. You might then switch to group-centered statements to elicit ideas and discussion. Ending the call with I-centered statements that specify any results, conclusions, or work assignments allows you to reestablish control of the proceedings.

Be aware of and use the power of language to ensure that your conference call achieves your desired goals.

-- *The 23 Minute Conference Rule*

A UK study revealed that the average attention span on a conference call is 23 minutes. After 23 minutes, the participants on your call start to tune out and do other things. This is the part where they start checking their email, sending text messages, or playing games. In fact, some people in the study admitted to falling asleep. When it comes to a face to face meeting, the attention span is increased to 35 minutes.

The study makes it clear that no matter if you're having a face to face meeting or hosting a conference call, you have to get to the point if you want the information to stick with participants. Here are three quick tips that you can apply to your next meeting so that you can say what you need to say while most people are going to be paying attention.

1. Use less time than you need. According to the study you have 23 minutes to say everything you need to say. When it comes time to actually plan out your conference, give yourself a little less time than what you actually have. This way, if you run over, you won't be extending the time too much. It's always better to end a little early, rather than ending very late.
2. Keep it short and sweet. A long drawn out introduction is only going to eat into the time that you

have to keep everyone's full attention. Instead of planning on a long introduction about the conference topic, send out an agenda ahead of time so that everyone already has a heads up. This way you can get right into the content.

3. Wandering minds will wander. No matter what you do to keep the attention of the group, there will still be people who are going to tune you out. Unfortunately, there isn't anything you can do about game addicts. Reach who you can, because you'll drive yourself crazy if you try to make a point to those who aren't paying attention.

When you only have 20-30 minutes to make an impression that is going to stay in someone's mind, you have to do what you can with the time allowed. Send out an agenda, plan for less time than you have, and remember there are some who will get distracted. What are you doing to stay within in the 23 minute time limit on your conference calls?

-- Conference Call Etiquette

Attending a boardroom meeting requires certain etiquette, as does a conference call. Below are simple tips to ensure that you and the others on the call get the most from the conversations and hold an effective meeting.

Before the call

• Disable the call-waiting feature on your phone.

• Inform your co-workers that you will be on a conference call so they don't enter your office making sarcastic comments for everyone to hear.

- Be on time. Don't disrupt the meeting if you arrive late. Wait until the end of the meeting to ask someone to fill you in on what you missed.
- Do not call in to the conference on a cell phone. Cell phones do not have consistently clear reception and this noise will filter into the entire conference.
- Sometimes you can't control where you are when you have to attend a conference call. If you are on the road and must use a cell phone, find a place where your signal is strong and pull over.

During the call

- Speak at a normal volume. Just because it's a conference call doesn't mean that your ability to be heard has decreased.
- Introduce yourself by saying hello and mentioning your name, location, and role. Also, each time you speak during the meeting, restate your name (e.g. "This is John in sales, and I feel that...")
- Do not interrupt others while they are speaking.
- It is polite to acknowledge the contributions people are adding to the call: "That's a great idea" or "Thanks for the information."
- Mute your line when you are not talking. This eliminates any distracting background sounds. The only time you need to be heard is when you are speaking.
- Be aware of all the distracting noises, such as keyboard sounds, chairs squeaking, and papers being shuffled, and keep them to a minimum.
- Do not put the call on speakerphone. Speaker-

phones pick up extraneous noises and have bad sound quality. The only appropriate time to use speakerphone is if there are multiple people in the room who should be included in the call. If this is the case, everyone sitting far from the phone needs to speak loud enough to be heard.

- Do not hit the hold button. You don't want the group to be serenaded by unnecessary music or irritating beeps.
- Do not do other work. A conference call needs your undivided attention and your respect for the other participants, just like a face-to-face meeting.
- Do not eat during the call.

These common courtesies are effortless and can make a conference call much more enjoyable if they are followed by all callers.

-- Six Tips for Leading an Effective Conference Call

When hosting a conference call, it may be difficult to lead and organize a large number of participants. These are simple, easy-to-remember tips that can improve time management, team building, tolerance, and communication while on a call.

Don't let anyone hog the speaking time. We all know that person who has a lot to say (either from too much coffee or too much solitude; one can't be sure of the cause), and he or she goes on and on about little details that everyone else feels are a waste of time. Try giving speakers time limits, such as ten minutes for presentations and two minutes for commenting on a conversation, and then it's someone else's turn. (On the other hand, some non-talkative teams would love to get anyone to talk for more than ten minutes!)

Don't react rashly. Sometimes hot topics come up while in a conference, and it is up to the leader to make sure all participants remain respectful in their comments. If the conversation veers off-course, be decisive and gracious in rerouting it back to the meeting agenda. Respectfully remind everyone that they are in a professional meeting and their comments need to reflect that.

Try to speak to everyone. Sometimes a conference takes place in a room full of people from which several members dial in. On those occasions, it's hard for callers to hear a conversation that goes on away from the microphone. If you're ever in a room with multiple people on the phone, try to make sure everyone speaks clearly and that the callers can hear the person speaking.

Communicate conference changes and updates. I can't tell you how many times I've dialed into a conference, only to find that the time, or even the day had changed. Make sure everyone attending the conference knows ahead of time if changes have been made. Sometimes it may become necessary to get replies from team members, just to be certain that they are aware of the changes. Also, if you're sending out notes or outlines that are needed during the conference, make sure to do this far enough in advance that everyone can access them easily for the call.

End when you promised. Employees appreciate respect for their time (even if they're on the clock working for you) as much as you appreciate their showing up to work on time each day. As much as you need the conference to begin on time, your team needs it to end on time. Days are busy, and people plan other work, out-of-office appointments, and other calls around these conference calls. Be respectful of everyone else's schedule.

Follow up in writing. Note who has been tasked to perform which activities. Good follow-up ensures that the plans you have discussed will be implemented, and that team members can be held accountable for specific tasks.

-- Office Conference Etiquette

When conferencing from your desk and lost in your full-steam-ahead mindset, you could be bothering others trying to work around you. Here are a few ways to be polite the next time:

If at all possible, take your call in a private area, even if all your conference rooms are filled. Not only will this cut down on the possibility of disturbing your neighbor, but you'll also be separated from distractions like IM, email, and games.

Let the people around you know you're going to be on a conference. Tell your buddy at the desk beside you that you may not be as fast as usual to respond to emails or IM.

Resist the urge to put the call on speakerphone. The people around you weren't invited to your conference, so they don't need to hear it. If you want to be hands free, do that with a headset.

Speak in a normal voice on the conference. Just because it's a conference call doesn't mean that your ability to be heard has decreased.

Make a funny sign to hang on your cubicle wall to let everyone know you're on a conference. Monsters and zombies are pre-approved by yours truly.

Having a conference call from your cubicle can be a distraction to your everyday work environment. We're used to going into conference rooms and being able to block out everything. But that's not always a possibility, so we have to be able to keep ourselves focused, as well as not disturbing our office neighbors.

-- Tips for a Brainstorming Conference Call

The scene of a company brainstorming session is a messy one; crumpled papers, half-eaten pastries, coffee cups, and exhausted people. But with the arrival of conference call, brainstorming participants are now often scattered about the country. Here are five tips that can make a teleconference brainstorming session productive:

1. After you have introduced the subject, allow everyone some time to think and write down ideas before the conversation begins.

2. Don't allow harsh comments while the ideas are being tossed around.

3. Encourage participants to offer any idea, even if it's a bit outrageous; it could inspire someone to have a great idea.

4. Continually vote on the ideas, eliminating those that receive little support. Eventually the winning idea will emerge.

5. Finally, bring new people into the call. Allowing a team member to call into your brainstorming session will bring new perspective to the process and could help stimulate the conversation--especially if they jump in when the rest of the team is stuck.

-- *International Conference Call Tips*

The English language is used throughout the world, but when you have conference call attendees for whom English is their second language, you need to keep some tips in mind to communicate effectively.

Americans are known as fast talkers. Slow your speech so the ESL, English as a second language, folks won't get frustrated or misunderstand your words.

Don't sprinkle your speech with metaphors or jargon. If you say, "He let the cat out of the bag," non-Americans may wonder why you put a cat in a bag in the first place.

At appropriate times, ask the international participants if they understand everyone's comments and if they have any questions. Sometimes it might be appropriate to hire an interpreter to assist during the event.

Be careful with humor. You may say something that is considered offensive in other cultures, and those people may lose respect for you.

Finally, be on time. In some countries, being just a few minutes late is an insult.

-- *Different Ways to Improve on Bad Conference Call Habits*

Though phone technology has improved steadily over the years and has simplified the way we communicate, old habits tend to linger. The following are common conferencing habits that call for improvement.

"I'll have to ask about that and get back to you." How many times have you been on a call and didn't know the answer to a question you were asked? In that situation, you might be running around the office, trying to find your solution, but wasting valuable time. Instead, start a conference call with the person you were speaking with and bring in the person with expertise. Then all questions can be asked and answered, and decisions made, without your being in a panic.

Don't worry, just auto record. If you're like most of us, you like to remember what was said during an important call. But sometimes, writing notes isn't the best option. Let's face it, when we try to take notes, we don't always remember to write down everything. And sometimes, writer's cramp can get even the best of us. The solution is to have your call recorded. You can even have it recorded automatically so you don't have to remember to start the recording. It's already done for you.

To mute or not to mute? Everyone should know how to mute and unmute the phone; this can be a person's best friend during important conference calls. Not only does the mute button cut background noise, but it also avoids embarrassing situations such as snoring (believe it or not), squeaky chairs, kids running in the background, and the list goes on and on.

Using a group mute will let you mute all the participant lines, leaving only the moderator and speaker lines open to speak freely. This will give you control over who speaks and when to allow a question-and-answer period in an orderly fashion. If you're recording your call, you'll get a clear recording without all the background noise included.

As you make these improvements to your calling habits, you'll see just how effective your conference calls can become.

-- Get a Headset for Your Next Conference Call

Don't you hate to be on speakerphone? Hear static and poor connection noise in a conference call? Put yourself in your listeners' shoes, and make sure the technology you use is helping to transfer your message with the minimum of distractions. Consider a headset for your next conference call.

A headset allows you maximum freedom, yet keeps the microphone close to your mouth and minimizes external noise that participants might hear from your end. Many great headsets are available and comfortable to wear. Many also have noise-canceling features that filter external noise and keep your call crystal clear. Plantronics offers a selection of moderately-to-premium priced headset/ telephone combinations from which you can choose to meet your conferencing needs.

If you are web conferencing, you will want to keep your hands free for accessing computer applications, opening documents, or note taking, and a headset allows you to do so while still delivering great sound quality.

-- Speakerphone Dos

As convenient as a speakerphone can be, it may not be the best choice for a conference call. Rather than repeat what you shouldn't do, however, let's talk here about good speakerphone etiquette if you do use it for your next conference call.

Sound check. Think of it like this: You're standing in a conference room and speaking in front of a crowd of people. You sound great. But if you were to take a megaphone, press your mouth against it, and speak in the exact same tone, your voice would sound distorted. A megaphone amplifies your voice, and a speakerphone works the same way. So before that next conference call, call into your conference line with a co-worker and do a sound check. Adjust your volume levels and distance from the microphone to get the best sound possible.

Location, location, location. It can't be stressed enough that using a speakerphone is going to pick up everything around you. It's even going to pick up your own voice bouncing back into the speaker. The smaller the room, the closer the walls, and the louder your voice, the more sound will reverb into your speaker, which could cause problems with feedback or echoing.

Wait to join. Enable speakerphone only after you've successfully joined your conference. Remember when you were a kid and put your face by a fan and said, "Luke, I am your father"? The movement of the air by the blades distorted your voice, didn't it? Well, a speakerphone will pick up the most subtle of movements in the air. Like your voice blowing through the fan, the sounds of the buttons you're pressing can get distorted. So enter the digits for your conference call before putting your phone into speaker mode.

-- *Conference Call Mute Is Never On*

On a conference call you can guarantee that someone is going to forget to mute their phone. There are a million stories out there of how people have heard bathroom visits, fast food orders, or worse. These interruptions are embarrassing, not only for the person responsible, but also for the host of the conference call.

Once, as an operator on a conference, I was dealing with a client who was going to have some high-profile people on their conference. The client expressed to me that it was important that there were no background interruptions on the call. I explained that all the participants would be muted, but since there would be about seven people on with the special speaker code, those lines wouldn't be muted. I suggested they use our star feature to mute the call and even had everyone test out the function to make sure they understood how it worked.

Inevitably, when the call started and one of the high-profile guests was speaking, my client's line was not muted and I suddenly heard the announcement that train #356 to Boston would be departing in five minutes. I had to make the split second decision to put his line on mute so that the announcement did not interrupt the high-profile speaker on the call. It made me uneasy to have to do that, but I couldn't risk his conference being interrupted, and this is the exact reason why people elect to have operators on their conference.

Audio conferences can be tricky. They aren't necessarily hard to participate in, but there are a lot of things to remember, and sometimes it's the simplest things we tend to forget.

The situation I had brings up a great point about being on a conference – always assume your line is not muted, even when it is. You might be positive you've remembered to put your line on mute, but you never know when something could happen to your line. What if your moderator accidentally turns off the feature while you're explaining to your kids why chocolate frosting is not an appropriate substitute for paint?

Always assume that your line is live, and it's a good rule that can apply to audio conferences or video.

-- How Good is Your Memory?

There are some people who can recall almost anything they've ever seen or heard at the drop of a hat. These people have what is called an eidetic memory, also referred to as photographic. These special people could attend or host a conference call, remember everything that was said, and go on with their day. However, even these memory masters have a need for conference calls with a good recording feature.

One obvious reason for any conference call to be recorded is to know what was said, by whom it was said by, and in what order. If this was the only reason to use recording then the eidetic memory folk would have no need for it. So what possible use could they have for conference call recording? The simplest reason is that everyone with a photographic memory knows that the majority of the human race doesn't share their perfect recall gift.

We can only imagine how many times one of them has had that annoying conversation where they have to convince someone with a fuzzy recall of actual events or conversations about what really transpired. This will keep those without a photographic memory on task and know what was discussed in a meeting.

That's not the only reason they and the rest of the world would want to use recording. Getting away from the basic reason of sheer remembering, recordings can also be used to multitask. While being recorded in a conference call, you could make sure to summarize at the end and specify task items for teams and individuals in your company. You can have your meeting accessible for playback, or simply crop it down to the summary and upload it. Then you shoot an email to all involved letting them know that there is a recording available for call-in playback. They all call in individually, listen to your recording, know exactly what they are supposed to do, and they get on with their day.

Think of all the meetings, emails, conversations, questions, and misunderstandings you can avoid just by putting your exact words in a conference call recording. It's like a bit of eidetic memory for us all.

-- How to Put Your Conference Call Recordings to Use

Most conference call services now provide much more than the standard conferencing ability, like out-dial services and recordings. You should know if and how your provider charges for recording files. Once you've found that out, think about the different ways you can use recordings in your business. Here are some ideas to consider:

Podcasts. You can call in to a conference line, record a podcast, and then post it on your website.

Replays. Did you host a conference that had a better turnout than usual? Have those who attended your conference told others about it, and now they want to hear it for themselves? With a recording, you can provide a replay of the conference that has everyone talking.

Snippets. Take the same recording and edit the MP3 to leave only the most-interesting parts. Use it as a marketing piece to showcase the highlights of your last presentation and entice people to sign up for your next event.

Filing. Just keeping a record of a conference can be a good reference. If you review your files and find that you're getting the same question a lot in your conferences and presentations, you can consider what you're missing or what you might need to word differently.

Backup. Sadly, people do sometimes go back on their word. I once talked to a customer who had used a conference call to defend her doctoral dissertation. She was told she had a specific amount of time to make some changes and report back. When they later tried to give her a shorter deadline, she didn't have a recording to prove what they had originally said.

I always say that it's better to have a recording and not need it than to need one and not have it.

Part Two: How to Have Better Presentations

-- *Facing Your Fear*

The number one fear of the average person is public speaking. A commonly taught trick for kicking this fear is to picture everyone in the audience in their underwear. That just makes things seem awkward, and that's no way to overcome your fear. Here are a few more effective ways to overcome your fear:

Don't try to ignore the fear; that never makes it any better. You'll be much more productive facing it.

Take small steps. If you have stage fright, it's a bad idea to volunteer to speak at a large conference. Start smaller, like a chapter of a local business group or even your church. Get used to being in front of people before you really put the pressure on.

Remember that nervous people sweat. Sounds gross, right? Tough luck. Sometimes nerves can overshadow the power of your deodorant, and there's nothing quite as embarrassing as being "un-sure." You might think about wearing dark colors just to lessen your worries by one.

Eat something. It's easy to not eat before you do something you're afraid of, because you're a tightly wound ball of nerves. But if you don't eat, I promise you won't be happy. Don't pass out on stage.

Think positive thoughts about yourself. Don't focus just on your speech contents, but also on yourself. Are you having a good hair day? Are your shoes amazing? Did you buy a new outfit that you really love? It's all about confidence, and giving yourself a little boost will help you get out there and face your anxiety.

If you can overcome your fear of public speaking, you open all kinds of doors for yourself.

-- Overcoming Fears & Having a Little Fun

Recently, I finally broke down and watched the original Nightmare on Elm Street. I have had a long time fear of Freddy Kruger and being able to watch that film was a big step in my growth. When one of the movie channels premiered the 2010 remake of the film, my friend and I decided to watch it – with one, fun little twist. We built a fort in the living room. Not just any fort, an old school dining room chairs and blankets fort. It dawned on me, after I made it through the movie without hiding my face or screaming bloody murder, that there was one very important reason why. I took something fearful and I made it fun.

While Freddy is just one kind of fear, there are a lot of other ones that people suffer through every day. By injecting a little fun into those moments, you can save yourself a lot of stress and turn a moment that is usually filled with nail-biting anxiety into a moment of triumph. One of the biggest moments of fear for people can come from the idea of speaking in public. The fort helped with the fear because it was a fun distraction for us and when you have a fear of speaking, you can use humor to ease yourself through some of the little mistakes you might make.

If you've ever tripped over your own feet walking out to the podium, instead of looking horrified, grab the microphone and declare that the clumsy portion of the day is over and everyone can stop waiting for you.

If you've ever lost your place, admit it. When I was in New Orleans in March, I remember someone losing their train of thought and while the crickets filled the room, the presenter simply laughed and backed up the slides, admitting to everyone, "Don't know what happened there. Let's try this again."

If you've ever stumbled over your words, just declare a new word thusly written and encourage everyone to tweet out the new word.

There's not a person in that room that hasn't experienced their own bad presentation, so feeling bad over a simple stumble isn't doing yourself any favors. Recover from it and create a fort in your brain where the things you're afraid of don't matter so much. Just remember that the fort is a safe place where humor is the thing that will beat back your fears.

-- Presentation Skills from the Shy Kid

Back in junior high, I was so nervous in front of a crowd that when I had a choir solo in front of the whole school, I rolled the ends of my skirt so much that I almost flashed the audience. Mortified, I realized a socially awkward girl prone to fidgeting and embarrassment had no business putting herself on the line like that, despite my love of singing.

When I moved, I decided to build a new me, and my fear of speaking in front of people was the first thing I tackled. I got active in debate, and by the time I graduated college in 2005, I had majored in communications. Not bad for a shy kid, don't you think? Here are the presentation skills that I know are going to help you knock some socks off:

Never read word-for-word from a printed document or slide show. Start strong; come out of the gate with a relevant story that ties everything together. Let go of the podium and take down the last wall between you and the audience. It's a presentation, not a sales pitch. Be passionate, exciting, and make people want to know more. Be open for questions, and if you run out of time, give the audience a way to get ahold of you later.

The people who taught me these things know far more about presenting in front of live crowds than I do. But thanks to some of these things, the shy, awkward kid from South Carolina moved to Arkansas and now has a career in which she's comfortable and happy.

-- Public Speaking Anxiety

I'm sure a lot of us have some resolutions we are trying to live up to and trying to make happen. Whether your resolution is to lose weight, stop smoking, or overcome something that held you up in the past, I'm sure you have a set of goals to make your resolution happen.

If your resolution is to be a better public speaker, it can be hard to set goals that will help you reach what is, more than likely, an end result of making a public speech. Like all resolutions, the best thing for you to do is to set smaller goals that will get you more comfortable with the idea of being in front of people, before you tackle the idea of a long speech.

If you suffer from public speaking anxiety and want to overcome it this year, try starting small and working your way up the ladder of challenges. Here are some easy (free!) suggestions to starting down the path of conquering the anxiety.

Volunteer time reading books at an after school program. Not only is this a great way to spend your time, but you'll get used to reading aloud. You will learn the importance of pace, tone, and not to do the annoying robot voice that will put us all to sleep. Small children are also forgiving – so it's an audience that can be very easy to make happy.

Join an Online Forum. Joining an online forum will help you learn how to articulate your thoughts into a speech-like format. The great thing about forums is that you'll make connections with people you wouldn't usually come in contact with, and it can teach you how to speak up in a situation when you're dealing with people you don't know.

Watch other speakers. Attend free events at your local community college or university and watch how other speakers use the stage to their advantage. Take notes about what you like and what you don't, and then practice at home.

If you want to overcome this kind of fear, you don't have to run out and spend a lot of money on different kinds of books and DVD's. You can find some ways to get a little bit of confidence in your abilities right in your own backyard and never have to spend a dime.

-- Inspire By Overcoming Fears

There is a big difference between being "fearful" and being "nervous". When it comes to public speaking, someone who has stage fright might sweat profusely or revisit their breakfast before it's time for them to go on stage. I've even heard stories about people who stand too straight with their knees locked and just fall over passed out.

Personally, I'm a nervous speaker, probably borderline on the whole "stage fright" bit. It takes me a few minutes to get warmed up in front of a crowd, but once I start feeling some confidence, I am able to shake off the nerves. As important as it is to inspire your audience, you have to have some of that inspiration too; otherwise your speech won't have the same excitement-boosting factor.

Here are some tips on how to draw a little inspiration for yourself before you go out in front of the waiting audience:

You're out there aren't you? There are a lot of people who would be too scared of even agreeing to speak at an engagement, let alone being able to take that stage.

Say some good things about yourself. You are your greatest critic after all, so shut up the negative voice inside of you that wants you to fall off the stage or rip the seam in your pants. Instead, pump yourself up with some positive things – even if you only end up complementing yourself on your hair.

The night before your speech, do a dramatic reading of your speech. No, maybe your speech isn't MacBeth or Romeo & Juliet, but doing something really over the top can help you shake off some of those 'pre-speech' nerves. Plus it would be really fun.

Stop second guessing yourself. You've been preparing for this speech for weeks, or even months. So put down the notes, stop making changes, and trust yourself.

What kind of things do you do in your preparation to give yourself an extra boost of confidence? Remember that you have to believe in what you're saying if you expect a room full of people to believe along with you.

-- How to Be an Unforgettable Public Speaker

Believe it or not, you can make yourself an unforgettable speaker. You have an amazing opportunity to make memories with your audience before, during, and after the presentation. Here are some steps to making this happen:

Shake some hands. Arrive about an hour before you're scheduled to start speaking, and introduce yourself to people coming to attend your speech. Some of the best speakers I've seen can be caught circulating through the crowd well before they would need to be at the venue. Introduce yourself to others, and find out what made them attend and what they would like to hear more about.

Tell some jokes, and smile a lot. When you're in the middle of your presentation, be sure you're smiling. Make eye contact with individuals in the audience instead of staring stone-faced at the wall at the back of the room. Use some humor if you're comfortable with it and others have said you do it well.

Standing in front of a group can be intimidating, but you can eliminate some of the nerves by treating the audience like your friends.

Grab their attention. Easier said than done, right? But the fact is that you have only two minutes to make an audience pay attention, so you have to grab their interest right away. You might cartwheel onto the stage or fly in on a wire, dressed in a super hero costume. But if these aren't your style, you can also open your speech by telling a story or using a funny image as your first slide.

Move easily. The only time it's okay to do the robot is on a dance floor. While you're in the middle of your presentation, you should move around. Step out from behind the podium. Get in front of your audience instead of lecturing from the sidelines.

-- *Share Your Knowledge*

I came to love public speaking in my time on a debate team, during which I learned a number of valuable lessons. At one tournament, for example, one of my opponents was a really cocky guy. He was an excellent debater, but his loud and constant boasting meant no one other than his own teammates wanted to be near him. You could hear him a mile away, talking about how great he was.

When I went up against him, he beat me so badly that I swear I still have a bruise. In fact, I think he might have won that tournament. But the judging sheet we got later told a different story. He had scored low on courtesy points. Courtesy points are usually the easiest things to get, because all you have to do is be nice to your opponent. Part of my beating was that he had just verbally assaulted me (it was bad; I cried after), and the judge had noticed. Yes, he won, but that judging sheet taught me there is always someone observing you before you speak.

What you do and say before an event is just as important as what you say during it. People are going to be watching you, and there's a good chance they will jump at the opportunity to pick you apart. So when you're invited to speak somewhere, go with the intention of sharing your knowledge with other people and not talking ill of others or about how awesome you are.

-- Types of Presentations

When you're asked to present at a conference or event, you should begin by figuring out what you want to present and creating an outline. While making your outline, you also have to figure out what you want your audience to do after your presentation is over. Are you just trying to give them useful information? Is it one of those cases where you are trying to make a sale? There are four different types of presentations you can give and their purpose is to invoke different reactions.

1. Informative Speeches – These are the most common types of presentations and are used to present research. A student who is defending a thesis or a

non-profit group that did a research study will use informative speeches to present their findings.

2. Demonstrative Speeches – These will show you how to do something. In introduction to communication classes, these speeches are usually "How to" kinds of speeches and include different pictures and steps to the process.

3. Persuasive Speeches – This kind of speech is trying to change the way you think about a subject or issue. If you've come to a health conference you may find yourself listening to why you should change your eating habits or stop drinking.

4. Inspirational Speeches – These speeches are designed to move your audience. Also considered a "motivational" speech, this is designed to encourage participants to go after their goals, whatever they may be. Inspirational speeches will tell stories and the hope is that the audience will feel an emotional connection to the topic.

Remember the late Apple CEO Steve Jobs and the presentations he gave when he introduced a new product? He gave you information; he showed you how to use a new product, told you how to use the product to solve a problem, made you understand why you needed it, and closed by letting you touch and feel the product.

Steve was the best at letting the entirety of the speech answer all of the questions of the decision making processes.

In truth, the best presentations will embody a little bit of each type of presentation, but you can use a specific type to help move you along the right path.

-- *Public Speaking Excuses*

Not a lot of people practice before giving a speech. We make excuses for why we can't or won't do it. Let's debunk some of those excuses right now and see why you should always practice before you present.

Excuse #1: I'm a pro. Yeah? So are professional athletes, musicians, actors, and even acrobats in the circus. They still show up to batting practice and dress rehearsals. Getting paid to speak doesn't mean you're immune to wardrobe malfunctions or technology failures.

Excuse #2: I don't have enough time. Make time, plain and simple. You should never make a presentation when you haven't familiarized yourself with the surroundings or topic. You would never present on a subject you knew nothing about, so why would you make a presentation in a conference room or over a phone system about which you knew nothing?

Excuse #3: I have to travel to get there. Okay, that's understandable, but that shouldn't be an excuse for absolutely not practicing. Give yourself enough time when you get to the venue to at least walk around the hall or ask an event organizer if there is anything special you should know about the presentation hall. Don't blindly expect everything to run smoothly. Pad your schedule with at least 10-20 minutes of down time before you start.

Those are the three biggest excuses I hear for why people don't do a run-through before their conferences. But remember, the goal is not perfection; striving for that will only lead to disappointment. You should instead strive for confidence. Part of confidence is being comfortable. So practice doesn't make perfect, but it does make confident public speakers.

-- Get a Handle on Your Audience

Your audience can be as diverse as your department, your employees, your clients, your competition, your board of directors, or even prospective employees. How you prepare your message depends on who your audience will be. Here are some questions to ask yourself about your upcoming audience:

Who are they? Who are the key influencers? Who has the most direct power? Who has indirect influence (opinion leaders, potential allies, even those who just stamp approvals or route communications)?

What do they already know? What do they need to learn? What are their expectations and preferences?

What do they feel? What emotions will arise as they hear your message? What's their current situation? How interested are they in your topic? Is it low priority or high priority? How curious are they?

How can you persuade them? What's their probable bias, positive or negative? Are they likely to favor your conclusions, be indifferent, or be adamantly opposed? Is your desired action easy or hard for them? Will it be something they aren't interested in doing? Will it be a burden or a joy? Will they agree to your ideas with gusto or reluctance?

All these are things to think about before writing your speech. If you do, you will likely get a positive response from your audience. But CEOs and managers often put off speech writing until they have to do it, which creates poorly thought-out, badly written, and ultimately ineffective talks. Taking a bit of extra time to think through your audience and objectives will help you to create a speech that does its job well.

-- Presentation Exercises

It's just common sense that before taking a run, you should stretch your muscles. Before trying to write a novel, you should get a general outline for your plot. The point of a plot in a story is to have yourself ready to dive into your story. It's the same thing for a presentation. There are some things that you should do before taking on presenting in front of a group. Here are a few things I recommend you do before you step up to make your presentation:

First, find a quiet place to park yourself and review your notes and slides. Make any last-minute notes about things you want to cover. Finish your pre-game 30 minutes before the start time. While it might seem good to keep going over your notes until you walk to the microphone, remember from high school and college that reviewing again before the start of your test isn't going to help. If you don't know it by now, you won't, so give yourself a break.

Second, pump yourself up with some music before the presentation. Stick in your headphones and jam, or if you're with some people, pipe it out to them too. You'd be surprised how much a couple of your favorite songs can get you ready to go You're not about to race in a marathon, save the universe, or take on the world, but no matter what, it's still just as important to you that you do well

-- *Public Speaking & Presenting Basics*

As someone in a position of leadership, you have to get up occasionally and talk to your constituents or your employees about policy changes, new plans, the state of the break room after lunch, or whatever. For many, it's old hat; for some, it induces terror of the worst sort. In either case, you'll do a better job if you pay attention to some speech-making basics.

Consider your body language. Speakers who slump or walk with a wilted appearance won't garner much respect or credibility. Posture is poise. Stand up straight while you speak. You don't have to stand stock still the entire time. Move naturally while you emphasize your points; use hand and arm gestures, walk in short paces within your speaking space, etc. that emphasize the points you're making. If you're speaking in a personal setting, like a networking event, you'll want to lessen the distance between yourself and your audience.

Think about your vocal qualities. If you get really nervous, watch your breathing, and slow it as much as possible. Try not to fear silence. If you're between points and saying nothing, that's better than stammering "um, um, um" as you find your bearings. Slow your speech to a meaningful pace and enunciate your words. Don't speak so slow that it is putting people to sleep, but don't speak so fast that you cannot be understood. Hurrying and not speaking with clarity can sound like mumbling.

Consider your speaking environment. Take a look

around and get a feel for your area. What kind of space are you in? How will your listeners be seated? Will they be around a table, in rows or chairs, or around multiple tables? Figure out how far away you are going to be from the first group of participants. In a very informal setting, you'll want to get as close to your participants as possible.

Think about what you should wear. Is it a casual event, or should you wear business attire?

Keep these four points in mind the next time you speak to a group of people. Not only will you feel confident, your audience will think you look confident as well.

-- Presentation Time Limits

My dad recently called me in a mess of bubbling excitement, the likes of which I hadn't heard since one of his Little League teams was battling it out for a championship. A few weeks ago, he got a new job and was faced with presenting a proposal for something new to his company. He struggles with doing presentations, not because he's shy but because it's just not something he's had to do a lot. His brain tends to get ahead of his mouth, too, especially when he's bubbling with ideas. He called me for some tips.

The first thing I told him, based on what I know about his ability to ramble, was to set a time limit for his presentation. He had one hour in front of the bigwigs, and he wanted to make the most of it, but he had about 30 pages of information he wanted to cover. We had to whittle all that down to a presentation that would fit in a time frame that didn't seem like too much or too little. I recommended that he give himself enough time to cover what he wanted to say but leave time for questions. Since he was presenting something new to the company, it was important to allow extra time for the Q&A session.

Next, I told him to define specific points to cover, and make them the most important things. I recommended a journalistic approach. In his presentation, he should answer who, what, when, where, why, and how, and then let the conversation start. Stick like glue to the plan. When you make a plan and then veer off the path, people can see that your thought train has derailed.

One of the best ways to combat your train of thought getting ahead of you is to make the plan first and then put together your PowerPoint. The slides will stay on track with the flow of your speech this way. Don't try to write them at the same time, you need to know what you're trying to tell participants before you try to present it to them.

In about ten minutes, we had my dad ready to go, and after another 30, we had his PowerPoint knocked out. It took us only about an hour to get him ready to present to a Fortune 500 company. And the best news? They loved his ideas and gave him the green light on a major new venture.

-- *Communication Barriers*

I was at a conference recently and sat next to someone who was using her laptop. I have no idea how her keyboard survived. I could hear the keys begging for help as she slammed her fingers down upon them. I was surprised she didn't use her elbow to hit the space bar and just put the thing out of its misery. A lot of barriers to communication can arise no matter if you're speaking to one person or a thousand. Here are a few of the most common and how you can overcome them:

Self. Effective speakers know that a "me" focus turns off an audience. Audience members want to hear how what you know will benefit them. Sure, tell stories, but remember to always bring the focus back to them and how they can apply your experience in their business.

Environment. One of the quickest ways to lose your excitement about speaking is to be in a bad setup or venue. Check out your setup before taking the stage to see if you're comfortable. If something doesn't feel quite right, like the arrangement of the chairs, go ahead and rearrange or prepare yourself for that.

Noise. All noises can cause a distraction during a presentation. On a conference call you can easily mute the entire audience with a click of a button, but dealing with a face-to-face audience offers more challenges. You can politely ask that they turn off their laptops and cell phones, but we all know not everyone is going to do that. You then have two choices, ignore them or embrace them.

As a speaker, it's important to anticipate the barriers to communication and how to break through them. And remember: Your keyboard never did anything to you. Try not to hurt it.

-- *Keep Your Audience Focused*

I have two cats, and as cats are prone to do, they get into things they shouldn't. The other night, as one of my little beasts poked her nose around an electrical outlet, the glare on my face did nothing to dissuade her from her exploration. It wasn't until I waved my hands in a large gesture and made a sound like air leaking from a tire that she paid attention to me. The lesson I learned was that if I want my cats to listen, I first have to get their attention.

In a lot of ways, your attendees at a speech are the same way. So how do you get their attention? Try three things that cat owners do.

Use big gestures. Stepping in front of a crowd means you have to command their attention. People are going to do their own thing unless they have something to pay attention to. You get their attention by grabbing it right away. You have two minutes to make people sit up and pay attention, and then you've lost them to their laptops or smart phones.

Give them treats. When my cats do something good they get a treat, maybe some cheese or a can of wet food. Throwing your participants an added bonus is going to make them stay focused and hang on your every word, just in case they might get another treat.

Don't be afraid to get their attention. Most cat owners know the wonders of the squirt bottle of water. Cats hate water, and it's the quickest way to get their attention. While I'm not advocating pointing a Super Soaker at the crowd and going crazy, I do think you need to figure out whom you're speaking to and get their attention in a way that's appropriate. Try asking the audience questions to keep them engaged. Use visuals to make the presentation interesting.

Hopefully, when you're done, your participants will have the resolve not to wind themselves around your legs in excitement.

-- How to Regain Audience Attention

Most of us who have given presentations have had at least one moment when we could feel the audience's attention slipping through our fingers. What can you do when this happens? You don't have to hurry to the end or pack it in. There are things you can do to bring them back under your spell. The Eloquent Woman blog has some good tips for this.[1]

Get out into the audience. All right, so you can't do this literally, but once the audience has mentally put you in a box, they pay attention quickly when you step out of it and walk around the room. You can do the same with your web cam. After 15 minutes of showing your head and shoulders, why not tilt the web cam, stand up and step back, and show your full body while you talk? It's different, more dynamic, and will wake up a few participants.

Gesture. Gestures help focus your body language to fully support what you're saying. And again, a gesture here or there will help break up the monotony of just your head talking. Of course, on a videoconference you need to stay aware of what can and can't be seen on screen, and remember to keep movements a little slower and smoother than normal to avoid blurry or choppy video.

Get the audience involved. You can talk about your chosen subject for hours, but never forget that the point of your presentation is to educate the participants. At random times, it's good to stop and ask questions. You can ask specific people (waking up all the others) or ask the group in a poll. A versatile part of a web conference is the chat feature. Encourage people often to type in their comments or questions so you can stop to give the answer, or work it in on the fly.

1 http://eloquentwoman.blogspot.com/2008/12/what-to-do-when-youre-losing-audience.html

-- Prepared Spontaneity

One thing that makes a speech livelier is natural flow. But how can you avoid a canned speech while making sure you're still informative? Lisa Braithwaite answers this question in her blog posting "Can you be prepared and still be spontaneous?"[1] Well, can you? Yes, you can; here's how:

Write a basic outline. As soon as you can, sketch out your main points and supporting ideas. Add enough information to this outline to be coherent, but not so much that it becomes a speech. Then leave it alone for a few days (or weeks if you have the time), occasionally returning to go over what you've written. This cements your main points and concepts in your mind so that you won't have to refer to an outline or written speech during the presentation. You'll sound as natural and confident as if you knew the subject by heart. Guess what—by then you will.

Research the audience. You want to know what your audience knows about your subject so you can fill in the gaps. Going over things they already know, or starting in the middle of a subject they have no clue about, are two great ways to lose your audience fast.

Have additions. While you're periodically going through your outline and notes, start marking places where stories, props, examples, and audience participation could go. As you become familiar with the natural flow, you'll know exactly where to slow the pace with a story or emphasize a point with an example.

Practice for time. Now when you talk through your presentation, including additions and places for audience questions and such, time yourself. However, don't have the clock staring you down. Start a stopwatch and then go into another room to practice. Naturally and without pressure, recite your speech. It may be over or under your time limit, but at least it won't sound canned. Edit your outline and notes to end on time.

Be prepared. After all your hard work, when you show up to speak you should need only a page or two of your outline, complete with reminders of good places for your additions and any other important information you need to convey. The outline is sparse and the notes are absent because all that information is in you. Start talking and let your presentation flow out. Your audience will appreciate your hard work.

1   http://coachlisab.blogspot.com/2009/02/can-you-be-prepared-and-still-be.html

-- 3 *Ways to Inspire With Honesty*

I won't go into too much detail, (because it's not my place to share for others, only myself) but I get to have a wonderful experience where a group of people talk to others and share some heart wrenching stories and memories. I was at one such event where I realized that one of the quickest ways to get an audience's attention is to be honest.

What does that mean though? Telling you to "be honest" is sort of like telling you to write "great content". It's a great tip, but there's no real substance to it. How does one "get honest" with a group of strangers? It can be an awkward thing to get up in front of people and tell what you might consider to be "too much".

Here are three ways you can tailor the honesty approach to presenting a topic to a more business-oriented audience:

Tell a story. Give your audience the inside scoop of where your idea or inspiration came from. Don't be afraid to tell them that you were sitting on your couch eating ice cream and watching Jersey Shore when a light bulb went off in your head. Share the little things that can make a member of your audience relate to you.

Don't be afraid to admit you were wrong. Life and business are the same in the sense that they require you to learn lessons along the way. Standing up in front of a group of people can show that you've been through the ups and downs, just like they have, but you were able to bounce back. When we're going through something difficult, we often feel like we're going through it alone. Hearing someone else's struggles can inspire in a heartbeat.

Emotion is passion. Loving something – be it a person, product, discovery – doesn't make you a bad business person. Why take on a project if you don't have passion for what you're doing? Getting up in front of an audience and showing your emotion toward something doesn't mean anything other than the fact that you're in the right place.

It's very easy to get up in front of everyone and be honest, but it's not a tactic we take to a credible presentation. We think that by admitting flaws or showing how much we believe in a thought or idea is a weakness in front of a group of people. In truth, it could be one of the best ways to make a great impression on our audience.

-- Failures and Success

When asked to make a business presentation, failure is usually not the kind of topic you want to focus around. Many times you're going to be presenting to a group of people who have paid to see you talk about your chosen subject, and when someone pays you to speak, it's doubtful that they want to hear anything else other than the moment that you succeeded.

History would disagree with that line of thinking. History would show you that failure is just another step towards success. History tells you that a better story is made by admitting your failures and telling your audience how those failures lead you to success. Here are three other people that would tell you failures matter and why.

"If you're not failing every now and again, it's a sign you're not doing anything very innovative." – Woody Allen

Failure makes for progressive thought and actions. With failure, we learn how to create and push the boundaries of what is commonly accepted as normal and how to push the boundaries of what can make things great. If we refuse to fail, then we refuse to grow.

"Failure is only the opportunity to begin again, only this time more wisely." - Henry Ford

Believe it or not, failing at something can be a light at the end of a tunnel. Whether it's a business venture or something you tried personally, it's not always about being perfect. Sometimes, it's about taking small steps, sometimes the wrong ones, to make you wake up and realize that you need a change or to try something different.

"I have not failed. I've just found 10,000 ways that won't work." – Thomas Edison

Moving a good idea to a great idea sometimes means you have to look back at a failure and see what you can do differently. There can be a very simple piece of the puzzle missing that can turn your failure into success. Apple is the perfect example of a company that used a failure to find a better plan. Remember the MessagePad (AKA The Newton)? Without that failed device it's possible that we would have never had the iPhone.

Not all failures are bad, just like not all successes are great. You can inspire an audience with admitting your failures just as quickly as you can by expressing your successes. Failures are truthful and human, and when we try something, it's not always the outcome we want at first. The inspiration is in the story and how you learned.

-- Did We Mention Being Honest?

There are a lot of important things when it comes to public speaking, and while the inspiration is one of those things, it definitely doesn't even begin to touch on everything. It doesn't change the fact that inspiring your audience and making them want to get up and embrace your ideas and practices will equal success.

Methods, figures, charts, whatever, sure they are there to help to show an audience how your practices can be incredibly useful. However, if you're not lighting a fire under them to make them get up and want to go and do something, then it's not going to do any good for you to stand up in front of them and lecture.

We all have different quirks, things we enjoy, and they have affected our business experiences. While "be yourself" is a great tip, it's another one of those things that doesn't really tell you anything.

What qualifies as "being yourself?" If it's getting up in front of your audience and acting like a clown because you enjoy playing pranks and making jokes, you're not going to be perceived as much of a serious business person. It's a careful balance between showing your personality and airing all your dirty laundry.

Tell stories that have personal meaning, but keep your stories appropriate for your audience.

Connect with your audience in a way that makes you comfortable – and doesn't cross boundaries. Walking up to a stranger and wrapping them in a bear hug is probably not a great idea. Best connection strategies? Good solid eye contact and a firm handshake.

Let your personality shine! There is something special about you that everyone should get to have a little taste of. If I was in front of an audience, I'd be making jokes about being short and confessing silly mistakes that I've made.

Before your next presentation, think about what sets you apart from the rest of the people that could have been invited to speak, and incorporate those parts of yourself into the presentation. Don't forget to be honest, kick your fear to the curb, and just have a good time.

-- Ten Tips for Turning Off Your Accent

When I was five my family moved to South Carolina and to this day, my mother likes to remind me of how she used to catch me practicing my southern accent in the mirror. The longer I've spent in the South, the more of an accent I've developed. I think I speak eloquently, but when I'm nervous, angry, or around friends and family, I do have a bit of a southern twang. I've been working on reducing what I call Southern Girl-itis. Here are ten quick tips for toning down or getting rid of your accent.

1.   Remember that it won't be easy; you're basically

teaching yourself how to speak again.

2. Identify words that give you a hard time, and practice them in a mirror.

3. Record yourself speaking to another person, or read a passage from a book. Play it back so you can spot letter combinations that might be giving you trouble.

4. Speak clearly by remembering to open your mouth.

5. Say the word in your head before you say it out loud.

6. Hold your fingers at the side of your throat when you speak to help yourself feel what shapes you're making when you say the words.

7. Immerse yourself in speech that doesn't showcase a regional accent.

8. Speak to someone with a different dialect (like someone from above the Mason-Dixon Line if you're combating a twang), and let that person tell you which words sounded "off."

9. Learn new words and expand your vocabulary to introduce your brain to words without an accent.

10. Remove colloquial terms like ya'll from your daily usage.

Whether you're like me with a country girl twang or you sound like a Boston Brahmin, using these tips will help rid you of your accent.

-- How to Debate Effectively and Rationally

On the night of November 3, 2010, I watched the election coverage on TV. I saw that a lot of the panel members on various news organizations couldn't hold a meaningful debate. They were rude, inappropriate, and downright mean. I'm a huge supporter of healthy debate, civility in discussion, and above all, being passionate about what's being discussed. If you're not passionate, why talk about it? But somewhere along the way, we've forgotten how to have a civil conversation with others we might disagree with. Here are nine tips to consider before engaging in healthy debate:

1. Be prepared. Don't be surprised when the passion from both sides bleeds through.

2. Let the other person finish. Interrupting makes you look like a jerk.

3. Consider your response carefully. Think about what you're about to say before you fire off at the mouth. You can't take it back once you say it, so don't say anything you'll regret.

4. Have respect for the other person's opinion, but don't concede your own.

5. Listen intently. Healthy debate is not just about making yourself heard; it's also about hearing someone else.

6. Try to see things from the other side. Before you respond, consider what the other person has said and what his or her motivations might be. You don't have to agree, but everyone is capable of understanding the other perspective. It should be about discussing opposing points of view and learning from each other.

7. Answer follow-up questions. If the person you're speaking with asks you a direct question, answer it. He or she is engaged in the conversation and wants to know more about your feelings.

8. Be passionate, but be polite. Name-calling and generalizations only make people feel attacked. You can have passion about your point of view, but never resort to name-calling. You're not eight, and this is not the playground.

9. Shake hands. At the end of every debate, shake hands and take a moment to converse about something that's not debate related. Talk about something you both agree on.

Debating with a person who opposes your views is hard, but when you're a grownup, it should be possible to sit down and talk about things with others, no matter what their opinions. Some of the greatest ideas in the world have been born from healthy debate, and there's no reason we should not talk about something just because we disagree.

Part Three: Making Communication Work

--Are Your Emails Clear?

Email, texting, and chatting are very popular forms of communication, but these written forms of communication do something that we weren't expecting when we embraced them with open arms.

They are hurting our ability to deliver clear messages.

In our company, email is a very popular form of communication. We email customers and co-workers to stay up to date on customers and answer our client's questions. It's important that everyone in our company knows how to write a great email, but I've noticed lately that some messages are getting lost in translation. When you remove elements from communication like tone and non-verbal signs, things become more open to emotional interpretation. Since how someone says something is just as important as what they actually say, email can cause more problems than it means to.

To make sure that you're communicating effectively when using email, be sure to embrace these suggestions and start applying them to your emails immediately.

When In Doubt...

Have you been emailing with a co-worker or customer a couple of times and there are still questions? Make your last email say something like: Is there a good time that I can call you to go over this? Like I said, we communicate with our customers through email and many times they need instructions on how to use some of our different features. If a customer has to email us twice to get the answers to their questions, we pick up the phone and give them a call. It is as simple as that.

Get a Second Opinion

There may be a chance that your email needs to send a stern message. Most often this occurs when you are the customer and you're trying to make your point clear. Just be sure to have a friend or someone else check the message over before you hit the send button. Being stern is one thing - being a jerk is another.

Ask for Confirmation

When making plans to meet or set up a conference call, be sure to ask the other party to confirm the date and time selected. A simple "Just let me know if that works for you" or "I'll look forward to seeing / speaking with you then" can cut down a lot of confusion on who is going to start the call or if it's even a good time for all the people involved.

Email is not a perfect form of communication and when you're communicating in writing, you lose a lot of the other clues in your communication strategy. Be sure you're writing clear and effective emails to your customers, co-workers, and your friends.

-- Delivering a Message to Individuals

Anyone who is ever a leader will have to sit down and talk with an employee face to face over a business issue. It could be a lot of things – maybe they need some extra direction, maybe you feel like there has been a lot of stress, or the employee has initiated the visit in the first place.

Speaking with an individual comes with different road blocks than addressing a group. The individual will have a different communication style, a way they like to be told things, and varying thresholds for their emotional tolerance. While, yes they are the employee and the discussion you're having may or may not be to reprimand the employee – you still want to at least be conscious of some of the details that you're about to bring up with them.

Communication is always a two-way process and if the person across from you feels like you're "lecturing" and not "communicating" they are less likely to listen to the helpful things you might be saying. Here are some tips on how to prepare yourself for a one on one conversation with an individual so that you can keep those lines of communication open.

Prepare how to communicate. Clarify the goal of the conversation – are you meeting because they requested the sit down session or are you going to have a staff meeting? Plan the meeting carefully before you ever sit down with the other party.

Strong delivery. No matter what you message is, you want to be sure that you deliver it in a matter that expresses your meaning with conviction. If you're trying to motivate an employee you want to make sure they understand that you believe in what they can accomplish.

Listen. Remember that communication is a two-way street, so you need to be willing to listen and understand what the person is saying.

Receive and evaluate. Process the message that your employee is sending you and then confirm the understanding. Once you're sure you have it right you can start to get into constructive parts of the conversation, like ways for improvement or changes that could help the business grow.

You need to make business communication personal to the individuals you're speaking with. In order to get through to someone or encourage them to come forward with ideas, they need to be invested in what you're saying.

-- Delivering a Message to Clients

In the same vein, a business communication problem may crop up if clients can't understand what you're trying to say. All the personal and two-way conversations in the world won't help if you're not making yourself clear. A few business-friendly tips to keeping it clear:

Define terms. If your clients won't know the acronyms in your business, don't keep throwing them around without explanation. If you're a stockbroker and your new wealthy investor does not know what an ETF is--exchange-traded fund--how will you convince her to let you put her money into one? Your marketing communications and documents given to clients need to have the definitions spelled out as if no one has a clue. Yes, even easy ones like the FBI or CIA. When in doubt, spell it out.

Don't recite a list of features. If your company has been in business for five years and can provide 20 different services, listing all those may cause your customers' eyes to glaze over. How about explaining how your services will ensure they never have to worry about their heating and air conditioning service again? How about promising that the years of experience guarantee the service personnel will arrive on time or the service call is free? (Yes, I'm dreaming, but wouldn't that be nice!) Make sure your best attributes are there, not for you to look and feel good, but so that your client looks and feels good. See the difference?

The shorter, the better. Some of the best marketing I've seen is short and sweet. A quick tag line summing up just what the client is looking for. Our business is a good example – we provide a number of different conference call features and services, but in the end, our marketing message is very simple. *We Connect People.* We determined what we provide to clients and shortened it to create our marketing message. Find out what your clients want and then keep it short.

Communicating to clients can be a daunting but it's not hard to take a "sales" message and turn into something that your customers can support. If you're looking to shorten up the message to get to your clients quicker you need to make sure that you can see things from the client prospective. One of the things that we do is to have all of our new employees go through the website and make a list of the parts of the process that could be confusing for customers. This helps us to go back, evaluate, and change the message if we need to.

--Communication in a Crisis

British Petroleum (BP) created a PR disaster with its handling of the crisis shortly after the oil spill in the Gulf of Mexico. If the PR team could hop in a time machine and go back, they would find a better way to handle things from the very start. (One would hope, right?) The thing about communication in a crisis is that you're probably dealing with that particular difficult situation for the first time, and it isn't until later that you can reflect on what happened and learn from mistakes as well as triumphs. This kind of communication can be especially difficult when hosting a conference call to update everyone and you have only your voice and your words to convey the messages.

Here are some important things to keep in mind when you have to respond to a crisis:

Express your emotions so there is no question about how you feel. Sometimes situations call for condolences to be expressed to families. Be sure you say that out loud. In a crisis, loss happens, and you're sorry for that. This is essential for when you're on a conference call, because no one can see your eyes to know if you truly mean what you say.

Use the tone of your voice to convey the seriousness of the situation. There's a time and place for jokes and humor, but this is not one of those. It's not always appropriate to try to "lighten the mood."

Use facts, and refrain from judgment or blame. When presenting information in a crisis, the last thing you want to do is speculate. Talk about or answer questions about what you know, not what you think.

Keep it simple and avoid using jargon. Word is going to travel fast once you hang up from the conference. Speak in simple terms to lessen the likelihood that your words and meaning could be twisted.

Be mindful of the words you are actually using. For example, using a word like promise is going to stand out. If you say "I promise" or "we promise" and you don't mean it literally, many listeners will still consider the promise to be chiseled into stone.

Remember that your words have so much power, even when you're just trying to offer comfort. In the end, what I've learned from BP and numerous other tragedies is that when it comes to communicating in a crisis, what people want most is reassurance, but as companies, we are also trying to give the public the facts.

--Communication Icebreakers

Have you ever found yourself preparing for a networking event and asking your friends for advice? How do you break the ice in a room full of people that you may not know or might not have anything in common with? It isn't always easy, but you can get through it. Here are five icebreakers that can help you make the most of your next networking event:

1. Arrive a little early. This allows for some extra time to get used to the new surroundings and familiarize yourself with the location. We're more relaxed in settings where we know our way around a little.

2. Be confident, not arrogant. When introducing yourself to people, remember there's a fine line

between knowing what you're talking about and sounding like a pompous jerk. Believing in yourself is one thing but walking around and pointing out all of your vast accomplishments for the sake of attention is another thing altogether.

3. Know the line and stick to it. Have a drink. I'm not a big fan of drinking outside my house in the first place, but limit yourself to one or two drinks at the most.

4. Stick your hand out and introduce yourself. Don't be afraid to walk up to someone and introduce yourself. The other person probably wants to meet people too.

5. Try to join conversations with your peers. Entering a conversation about a subject you're not interested in or don't have any experience with will translate into your being unconfident. Find people talking about something you know a little about and have passion for.

Those are five easy ways to break the ice at your next networking event. Remember, everyone is there for the same reason, to meet people and make connections.

--Useful Debate and Open Mind

Have you ever fallen into a conversation you didn't really want to have? I have a friend who is incredibly smart, open, and kind, but we disagree on 99.99% of everything socially and politically. There isn't anything wrong with that since she and I obey the rules for civil debate. Sorry to tell you, but not everyone is going to be able to have these kinds of open conversations. There is a fine line between openly sharing ideas and wanting to bang your head against the wall.

If we want to gain better perspective on the world we have to step out of our comfort zone and start listening to the opinions of others around us. How do we introduce ourselves to new ideas and opinions?

Attend an event outside of your comfort zone. Sign up to go to a networking event or conference that you wouldn't usually see yourself attending. If you're into social media marketing, sign up to attend a conference that focuses on more traditional marketing ventures.

Go out of your way to make a friend who has different opinions. The old adage of opposites attract can be very helpful when it comes to expanding your horizons. Making a new friend who loves comic books might show you that you don't have to be surrounded with the people who love and think the way you do.

Educate yourself on new things. Set a goal to learn about one new opinion each month. Think about the things you are passionate about; educate yourself on the origins of the "opposing side's" opinion. Why do they feel the way they do? How were their thoughts and opinions shaped by the changes in the world? Just remember to read with an open mind instead of a defensive one.

Learning another's opinion is an important part of success and just because you may not agree, it doesn't mean their opinions should be discounted.

The responsibilities that come with a leadership role include the capability of leading a meeting and being able to effectively communicate.   These two tasks ensure that the message of your meeting is understood by everyone involved with as little confusion as possible as well as with minimal interruptions.   Once you are able to master your communication skills along with your leadership abilities, you should find your meetings running much smoother and according to planned.

--Fight Meeting Blues

It's something we all have experienced and all dread: the really long meeting that goes nowhere and gets nothing done. Why do these meetings happen? They seem to be more about impressing someone's boss than they are about productivity. In any case, if you have the ability, please thwart long, useless meetings and replace them with something that will help rather than hurt.

When you think of a typical meeting, you might picture everyone sitting around a table comfortably in their chair.   The meeting might take a while to actually start because of small talk amongst the participants. You might have some people messing with their phones, not fully paying attention to what is being discussed, and asking to have the information repeated. If you want to eliminate this sort of meeting lag, then a great way to keep it short and to the point would be to have a "stand up" meeting. Have everyone stand around the table instead of sitting. This will make it hard for your participants to feel comfortable and will encourage the meeting to start and end on time.

A big tip for short, effective meetings is to not have a meeting. That's right: If you can accomplish the work through phone calls, conference calls, or emails, don't call a meeting. This is the same principle behind abolishing weekly meetings, progress meetings, and other such get-togethers that only exist because someone thought it would be good for "synergy" if everyone met regularly. The recurring meeting guarantees two things: Time will be wasted because there aren't enough items to cover, and someone will be frantically creating something at the last minute to look productive for the meeting.

Your caveat for meetings should be "less is more." This means shorter time lengths, of course, but also smaller groups of attendees. With fewer participants, people will be less likely to snooze or cruise through a meeting. You'll be able to notice the more-quiet attendees and ask for their input. When everyone works together, you get better results. Keep in mind, more people talking encourages digressions and other time wasters. Try to keep the meeting focused, even if it means interrupting someone as they go off topic.

If someone does happen to digress with an issue they feel is important, write it down and let them know you will arrange another meeting to address the issue. Also, if you have someone trying to make a point but it starts to turn into a monologue, don't be afraid to interrupt. Politely let them know their opinion has been heard, but the meeting needs to move forward. You can also offer for anyone who may have concerns to send you an email, and if needed you can schedule to meet at another time to talk about these issues.

Videoconferences aren't as real as, say, shaking some-one's hand, but they're effective when replacing unnecessary meetings. For a productive meeting, get the two or three people who are actually needed into a videoconference. They don't have to leave their desks, and you can conduct your business efficiently. And if you need assurance that the videoconference won't go long, have everyone pull back from his or her web cam and stand for the entire meeting.

--*Listening Skills*

In communicating effectively, nothing is more important than listening. Since we're surrounded by distractions, it's hard not to look as if you're completely ignoring the person. On a conference call or a phone call, it's even harder to seem engaged because no one can see you, making your listening skills even more important.

Here are some listening skills you can use to show you're engaged and interested in the conversation you're having:

Turn off email, IM, and even your phone. Even if you put everything on silent and turn the speakers on your computer down, people can hear you typing. You should give your undivided attention to the conversation, unless the conversation you're having online is directly related to the conversation you're having on the phone.

Repeat the question with your answer. When asked a question, try to repeat bits of it back in your answer. Let's say you are asked a question about the changing climate of business travel. You should respond with, "That's a great question. I think the changing climate of business travel is ..." This lets the person asking the questions know you're actively listening.

Let the natural flow of conversation take over. Keep a notepad in front of you. If someone is speaking for a long time, then you can jot down notes of things you might want to ask, keep track of good points in the conversation, or note things you'd like to comment on. This way, you're not interrupting the speaker, you're keeping your thoughts organized, and you're writing what you feel is important to discuss down.

Remember, conversations are nothing without active listeners. Using these techniques may improve your comprehension while listening. You might be surprised how much you can learn just by being engaged with the conversation.

--Master Your Voice to Captivate Your Audience

An often overlooked aspect of a presentation is your voice. A study conducted at UCLA by Dr. Albert Mehrabian found that when visual, vocal and verbal sounds are inconsistent, the actual content of your presentation counts for a mere 7 percent of the entire message. In other words, everyone is paying attention to what you do.

In fact, 55 percent of the message, according to Mehrabian, comes from your facial expressions and body language. The remaining 38 percent comes from your voice. Sure, it's less of a factor than your posture, your gestures, and your facial expressions combined, but mastering your voice gives your message a 38 percent better chance of getting through. With that in mind, here are some tips for improving your voice quality.

- Let yourself be heard…by yourself - Have you ever heard yourself on a recording and discovered that your voice sounded differently than the way you hear it in your head? That's because it does. Your voice enters your inner ear via vibrations in your chest, throat, and mouth. This is called bone-conditioned sound, because it hits your inner ear after traveling through the tissue of the head. All external sounds travel through the air, where they're dispersed, and then enter your ear. This is called air-conditioned sound. The latter sound type typically sounds less rich and higher in pitch. One of the best ways to get an accurate idea of what you sound like is to leave yourself messages or to speak into a recorder. You can try different things out and alter the pitch of your voice to get the best clarity.

- Animate Your Voice – Some people think it's best to sound casual when they speak. But if you sound too casual you may come off as dispassionate, monotone, or downright boring. Instead, focus on animating your voice, delivering key emphasis on important aspects, varying pitch and tone. With some practice your talks will become livelier, your audience more engaged.

- Physical Vocal Support – There are a number of physical things you can do to improve voice quality. You can sit or stand up straight, which ensures your airway is unhindered. Take deep breaths; the more

air the better. As you talk you can use your lower dia-
phragm to push the air back out, helping your voice
to sound clear and confident. You should also focus
on using the muscles in your tongue and mouth to
articulate the words correctly and avoid slurring.

Paying attention to the actual quality of your voice
is one of the best ways to captivate an audience. Though
it may seem tedious, taking the time to learn the above
steps is one of the best ways to improve your public
speaking.

--Filler Words Can Kill Your Leadership Authority

When speaking, many people fill the silences, breaks, and
pauses with filler words. These fillers can become habits
you won't seem to notice, but perhaps your listeners might.
Sometimes, it's hard to listen to ourselves speak and figure
out which filler words we have a habit of using.

A common filler word used primarily by teens is like.
They can pepper a simple sentence with like, sometimes to
the point that it's more than half the words used. Other
filler words include, but are not limited to; actually, you
know, but uh, and in any case. How many times have you
used any of these fillers in your last conversation?

If you've noticed a particular word or phrase filling
your sentences, you might be curious about how to banish
the space fillers. If you've already identified a filler, you're
doing great. But if unsure, ask a friend or record a conversation. Even better is downloading and reviewing the recordings of your last few phone calls.

Once you've spotted the filler, take notice of each time you use it, and try to choose a different word when you're about to say the filler. The best habit to form, however, is one of silence. When pauses occur that normally you would have filled, just let the silence happen. Not only will it vastly decrease the use of fillers, but your words as a whole will also have more gravitas and power.[1]

1 http://www.presentationmagazine.com/kill-your-fill-ers-before-they-kill-your-presentation-630.htm

--It Might Sound Right, But It's Actually Wrong

Sayings and turns of phrase used incorrectly can make you look bad. People treat you by how you dress and generally present yourself. On a phone call, when they can't see you, they judge by how you speak and what you say. With that in mind, let's look at some common words and phrases in everyday use and make sure you're saying what you want others to hear.[1]

First are words that are similar to another but mean different things. A common mistake is saying further when you mean farther, as in "further than I can run." Farther is the word that refers to actual, measurable distance. Along those lines, when you mean to say something is less than a specific number, you say "fewer than ten." Alternatively, you would say, "You have less than me."

A sneaky one is the difference between bring and take, and it all depends on which direction the item is going. If you are going to a party, you are taking the wine. The hostess of that same party can say you are bringing the wine to her.

My favorite is the subtle distinction between infer and imply. If someone suggestively says something, he or she is implying. If you draw a conclusion from someone's statements, you are inferring.

What about phrases we use almost without thinking? For example, some people say they need to "hone in on a solution" when they actually mean to say "home in." Or when they say that something is "different than" something else, it's more correct to say it's "different from."

Less is more in so many ways, and the same goes for speaking. One such way is to drop the of when combined with outside. The dogs aren't "outside of the house"; they're simply "outside the house."

I hope these speaking and usage tips will "raise the question"--not "beg the question"--of your verbal habits and help you vocally put your best foot forward.

1 http://www.bspcn.com/2010/08/25/24-things-you-might-be-saying-wrong

-- Meeting Icebreakers: The Best of the Best

It's one thing to talk about icebreakers in theory and another to think of them in practice. For most meetings in which participants are professionals, icebreakers that require actions not normally associated with day-to-day office behaviors generally make people uncomfortable.

Successful icebreakers for these groups usually consist of clustering people around a table and having them share memorable information, finding innovative ways to get them to introduce themselves to each other, or having them work collectively on a problem where everyone has to contribute. Below are some of the most-successful icebreakers we know.

Fact or Fiction: Have all at the table write down three surprising things about themselves, two of which are true and one of which is made up. Each person, in turn, reads his or her list, and then the rest of the group votes on which "fact" they feel is the "false" one. If the table does not correctly pick a person's made-up "fact," that person wins. A table can have more than one winner.

If you have more than one table full of people, have a competition between tables. Each table decides which of its winners should compete in the "finals." The selected finalists get up and present their "facts" to the whole group. Each table (except the one the finalist is from) has one vote to decide which of the "facts" is false. And at the end, the whole group votes on which of the finalists had the most-deceiving "fact." This helps people get to know and remember their colleagues.

Same/Different: Divide the group into teams of three or four, and give each team a large sheet of paper and each person a different-colored marker. Have each person draw a large oval such that each oval overlaps with the others in the center of the piece of paper. Give the group a theme that pertains to the meeting objectives. Tell people they have to write down at least five thoughts about the theme in the non-overlapping and mutually overlapping areas of their ovals. Give them five minutes, no more, to talk about their similarities and differences and write them in their ovals.

If there's more than one team, compare results and identify common thoughts in both parts of the diagram and what light these similarities and differences shed on the purpose of the meeting. This helps team members understand shared objectives and see, in a non-confrontational way, how their views differ from those on the team.

Brainstorm: Break the group into teams of four or five. Give them a topic. Pick one that's fun and simple, such as "What would you take on a trip to the jungle?" or "List things that are blue." Give your teams two minutes, no more, and tell them, "This is a contest, and the team with the most items on its list wins." Tell the teams to write down as many things as they can and not to discuss anything, just list things. This helps people to share ideas without fearing what other people will think.

Free Association: The goal is to have small groups or the team generate as many words or phrases as they can related to a particular topic tied to the meeting objective. Give the group(s) a key word and then give them two minutes to list, as quickly as possible, as many words or thoughts as pop into their heads. For example, if your company is trying to decide whether to reduce travel and increase the use of teleconferencing, you might use the word teleconferencing and have people list words or phrases associated with it. For example, they might say: "saves money," "saves time," "impersonal," "need to see other people," "get distracted," "sound quality," and so on. This reveals what people are thinking, similarities in viewpoints, and possible problem areas or topics that need addressing.

Nametags: Prepare nametags for each person and put them in a box. As people walk into the room, each person picks a nametag (not his or her own). When everyone is present, participants are told to find the person whose nametag they drew, introduce themselves, and say a few interesting things about themselves (birthplace, hobby, etc.). When all have their own nametags, they introduce the person whose nametag they were initially given. This helps people get to know and remember each other.

Desert Island: Group people in teams of five or six and tell them they will be marooned on a desert island. Give them 30 seconds to list all the things they will want to take; each person has to contribute at least three things. At the end of the time, tell the teams they can take only three things. Have the person who suggested each item tell why he or she suggested it and defend why it should be chosen. This helps the team learn about how each of them thinks, get to know each other's values, and see how each solves problems.

-- The Five-Minute Rule

No doubt you've observed that people arrive late for meetings. The other night we were monitoring our call volume, and we saw that of the hundreds of meetings held that evening, the majority had late arrivals. Specifically, 12.1 percent of attendees arrived early, and 87.9 percent arrived within five minutes of the start time. We notice this kind of trend when we prepare for our Operator Answered services. In fact, to make sure all of the late comers are joined into the conference as soon as they call in, all of our operators are readily available fifteen minutes after the call is scheduled to start.

What can we learn from this? The next time you hold a meeting, begin on time, but don't give out the "meat" of your presentation until at least five minutes in. We all know that life happens and sometimes you can't help but to be late on occasion. However, if you notice someone who is consistently tardy to your meetings, find out what their situation is and determine a solution to their tardiness. Also make sure to point out the importance of their making the meeting on time. State that you don't want them to miss vital information, however, you can't always put the meeting on hold to wait for their arrival as it would extend the meeting longer than scheduled. Knowing that you are concerned with their meeting attendance might encourage them to start showing up before the meeting actually starts.

-- Is There a Smile In Your Voice?

Dismiss the mechanical and physics issues and think about the underlying meaning. No matter what you do, who you are, or what your job title is, you still have to deal with people daily. Since you never know what opportunities are waiting around the corner, that smile should always be in your voice.

Sure, we've all fallen victim to the bad day syndrome, where we feel as if we're going through the motions. How do you kick that feeling and get a smile back in your voice? Here are a few things we do in our office to get a smile back:

We can be silly. We have this board on the office door where we remind everyone of important calls that day.

When a call is over, we write down funny things we heard or silly things we said during the call.

We're not afraid to take a break from our desks. Sometimes, when you just need to get up and detach for a second or two. Whether you stand up and stretch or take a walk around the office, it will help you take a breather and regroup.

We laugh. Everyone in the office gets along really well, and we don't have a problem taking a break to tell funny stories about things our kids have done or what our spouses have said. That bit of laughter helps us to decompress, even if only for a second. Laughter really is the best medicine.

--12 Ways to Get Motivated Right Now

This thing that we refer to as a "bad" day is really a personal choice to let the blues rule the day. It's human nature to feel a little down sometimes, but it still remains something that we can control.

When that day stretches into a few days or a week, there could be a bigger problem. We can see the light at the end of the tunnel, but it's hard to keep from getting lost in the darkness. You've been there, I've been there – so what do you do? Here are 12 ways that I refocus to get motivated.

1. Talk to your mom. (Also acceptable: talking to Dad) My mom gives the best advice and I love being able to sit down with her and just talk about things. Sometimes, my mom holds my hand and tells me those wonderful mom things like, "You're

so special". Other times, my mom tells me to get over myself – which is usually exactly what I need to hear.

2. Make a playlist. Grab yourself some new songs from iTunes or Amazon and make a list of songs that make you tap your feet and get excited. Listen to those when you're trying to get unstuck on a task.

3. Stop for a few minutes. Put down your pen or iPad and step away from the keyboard. Give yourself a clean five minute break.

4. Do something else. Stuck on a task? Put it down and come back to it later.

5. Make a list. When all your upcoming tasks are swirling in your head, it can feel a little overwhelming, so write them down. Cross them out as you get them done. You'll feel better.

6. Change the way you're trying to complete a task. Trying to write a blog post on your computer and it's just not working? Grab a pen and a notebook and try going that route. You'd be surprised how often I can be found jotting down notes or whole posts on a piece of paper.

7. Look at something positive. Go back and remind yourself of something that was challenging, but you were able to get through and come out on top. That can sometimes help you remember that you've been down this road before and you made it through.

8. Ask for help. Seriously, there's nothing wrong with this. I think we'd all be a little less frizzy haired and spend less time rubbing our faces if we could just do this a little easier.

9. 15 Minute Facebook break (No, seriously) Just do something to make your mind not think about work related things. Scroll your news feed and talk to a couple of people. Give yourself a little mental break.

10. Change your location. Sitting in the office trying to write a blog post? Grab your purse and go get some coffee. Change the scenery and get busy.

11. Go for a drive. Now, don't just walk out in the middle of your day at the office – that's going to have an opposite effect, I suppose. Instead, take a little detour on your way home. Or if you have the luxury to make your own schedule, just put some things on hold and get in the car. Roll down the windows, turn up the radio, and let go.

12. Turn off your electronic devices. Give yourself at least 30 minutes every day without a notification or email notice. The really bad thing about email notifications is that we feel pressured to respond right away. It's totally acceptable to read a book and relax when you're at home – the email will wait.

Hey, we all get the blues. I'm not immune to it, none of us really are – so what kind of things do you do to get yourself feeling, well, like yourself again?

--Tips for a Smooth Meeting

You might have had a meeting that started to get out of hand. You might have an assortment of unruly behavior; yelling, arguing, and topic hijacking. How can you run your next meeting in an orderly manner? Here are some useful tips:

Create a well-structured meeting. Have a written agenda that includes an objective. For example, agenda topic: the cost of doing business. Objective: strategies to significantly decrease costs. Having a structured meeting decreases the opportunities for arguments. Striving to meet the objective can make everyone feel like they are a part of a team.

Review the agenda. Prior to the meeting, offer attendees the opportunity to review the agenda and suggest additional items. By participating in the planning, attendees will be less likely to oppose you during the meeting.

Invite only those who must be at the meeting. People forced to attend unnecessarily might become resentful or pout during the meeting.

Encourage everyone to participate. Don't let the argumentative types dominate the discussion. As the meeting leader, have the courage to be firm with disruptive participants. Decrease confrontations by encouraging attendees to focus on the stated goals and not on evaluating the ideas of other attendees.

-- Leadership with Telecommuters

Telecommuting has some great benefits for your employees. It gives them the opportunity to work remotely from home as well as saves them the cost of fuel.

Your employees also have a better chance of balancing work/life balance. However, with the benefits also rise some concerns. The quality of work might suffer due to lack of in-person contact with colleagues, and your employees might become less productive due to lack of supervision.

To help eliminate these concerns, it's best to keep constant communication with your employees who telecommute. If possible, have them come into the office once a week to discuss their workload or any projects they might be working on.

Also, if you do notice a change in their productivity, then you might want to reconsider how many days they can work from home as opposed to working from the office. It's possible they might need a certain structure to perform at their best level.

To determine if telecommuting would benefit your business, review specific departments to see if their environment would allow them to work from home.

In most cases, you can allow call center representatives to work from home since their main priority would be to answer phones. Not only would your employees save money on their commute, but you would also save money by eliminating the desk space and office supplies that are usually needed to accommodate a call center. Positions that require clerical work or filing probably wouldn't benefit from telecommuting. Usually, the employee needs to be on site to file company documents since they might contain confidential information.

--Five Tips for a Happier Home Worker

Last year, we had an ice storm and record breaking cold weather that trapped most people in their homes for four days. I personally went a little crazy after two days and was ready to return to the office. I couldn't imagine how people do that kind of thing every day – then I realized they probably weren't thrown in to the middle of it like I was, nor are they sitting in front of their laptop in their living room because they don't own a desk.

That week taught me a lot about what it takes to work from home and the things that would have made my four days in my living room a little more productive and a little less crazy. Here are five tips to being a little more productive at home and a little less distracted:

1. Make a written schedule and include breaks. Plan out your day on paper and stick to it, but schedule yourself to have breaks away from your desk. I know you want to go change out a load of laundry – so put it on your schedule so it gets done and you can get back to work.

2. Have a daily conference call to check in with your employees or co-workers. When you're away from your desk and away from everyone, it can be hard to keep track of those that you work with. Check in with them daily and remind yourself of the people you work with.

3. If you have an office to go to, schedule a day in the middle of the week to spend the day there. If not, grab your laptop or iPad so you can get out of the house for a little while.

4. Shut the door when "work time" is over. Keep a separation between your work and home life by creating a work space that you can close the door to, that way, you won't see the stack of papers on

your desk that need to be finished. Out of sight and out of mind – enjoy time at home!

5. Work with background noise that makes you comfortable. Some people work better with complete silence. Personally, I need some background tunes. In the office, you'll rarely find me without my headphones on, and at home, I love the sound of the TV in the background. Take advantage of being at home and watch a violent slasher flick, if that's what motivates you – just turn it off before you take a call or have a video conference.

I know a lot of you work from home – it's a trend that we've seen on the increase over the last few years. As someone who probably wouldn't like it very much, I'm wondering if any of you ever felt the same. What did you do to make your day more productive at home? Did you hate it at first and now you love it? What happened to make you change your mind?

With the change of technology and communications, webinars are being used to update employees on policy changes or make sales leads. When leading these webinars, it's important that your communication skills are polished because many of the times, there is an element of communication (like seeing the other person) that is lost.

--Webinar, Webcast, Web Conferencing: What's the Difference?

Although their names are similar, webinars, web conferences, and webcasts are very different communication mediums, each suited for different audiences or messages. Webcasts are where audio and/or video content is streamed to many people over the Internet. Webcasts only allow you to hear and/or see what's being transmitted. There's no way to interact with the people transmitting the content. A good example is when a radio or TV station simulcasts its show over the Internet. A lot of companies use webcasting to make presentations for stockholders or potential investors.

Web conferencing is a fully interactive, live conference held over the Internet in real time. In a web conference, people sit at their personal computers and log into a host site, which generally has a wide variety of applications that can be used to display and share information as well as audio, video, and desktops. A meeting then takes place between the people logged on.

Webinars are a type of web conference, although many times they're a one-way transmission of information, generally including a slide show. But webinars are often designed to have elements of interactivity. Generally, in addition to logging on with a computer, attendees also call in on the phone as is done for a conference call. Via phone, the presenter discusses the information transmitted to everyone's computer screen, and participants can ask questions. Like web conferences, a webinar is live and has specific starting and ending times.

--*Building Rapport with Customers through Webinars*

Webinars have become trendy. But to entice viewers to sign up, as well as watch the entire webinar, you have to offer them plenty of value. If your invitation has the fingerprints of an aggressive copywriter all over it ("join this webinar or you'll regret it!"), you're going to decrease the number of attendees.

To engage and hold your audience, don't turn your webinar into a sales pitch. If you do, some people will be bored, while others will be resentful and will simply exit. It's not like sitting in a convention room and having to awkwardly walk out.

It has been estimated that less than 10 percent of people who participate in a webinar are prepared to sign on the dotted line. So don't focus on your specific products or services, and don't instruct your sales team to contact the audience immediately after the conclusion.

Instead, offer a presentation filled with interesting and unique information that will establish your company as an exceptional resource. This will create a rapport and trust with potential clients. The delighted attendees will then actually promote your webinar and your company to other potential customers.

--Scheduling Your Webinar: When Is the Best Time?

Because webinars don't require people to go anywhere, there's a lot of flexibility in scheduling them. Most presenters have not adjusted to this brave new world of freedom or the things they need to think about when scheduling webinars. So here are some tips to help.

Be sure the time for your webinar works with the time zone in which your attendees live. Depending on whether you're looking for a national or international audience, you may need to think about scheduling your webinar twice.

Believe it or not, industry surveys have found that if you're targeting professionals, Mondays and Fridays generally get good attendance. But these are bad days if your target is the support staff.

Also summer months and holiday weeks, like the beginning of the week of Thanksgiving or the week between Christmas and New Year's, can work well, though scheduling can again depend on your target audience. For example, if you're looking to attract delivery people, any time two months before Christmas is off limits.

Because other meetings usually begin and end on the hour, start your webinar at a quarter past, and end on the hour or an hour and a half later. This lets your attendees get back from their previous meeting and get ready, and it lets them finish your webinar before they have to get to their next meeting.

Try to avoid the lunch hour. The best times to consider are generally 10:15 A.M. and 2:15 P.M., because most people are already at work, no matter how late their workday starts, and your webinar will be over before those who come in early have to go home.

--Webinar Marketing: Getting the News Out

As technology has advanced, making online training simpler and more interactive, and as businesses and users become more familiar with online distance learning, the webinar marketplace has exploded. The webinar industry is expanding at a rate of 20-30 percent each year. Search engines that are already swamped with webinar offerings will soon be more than swamped.

How do you make your webinar stand out in the crowd? As we know, it's one thing to create a great webinar and another to reach the people who might want to take it, especially in the ever growing field of webinar providers.

Of course your company can always simply list the webinar on its website and hope people somehow find it and then are intrigued enough to click on the link and decide it's just what they've been looking for. But we don't recommend that approach.

It can cost big money to register for Google AdWords or some similar search engine pay-for-placement/click utility to shunt potential users to your webinar. But did you know you can get great visibility by sending out a press release through Business Wire, PR Newswire, or Market Wire? Releases to these news providers sometimes gets picked up by search engine news sites like Google, MSN, and Yahoo News. And the cost is a generally very reasonable flat rate, plus it stays visible to search engines for 21-28 days.

Every day, companies and executives surf these news sites using industry keywords to find articles of interest. If you word your press release right, you could reach your intended audience more quickly (and cheaply) than you might guess.

Not every press release is created equal, at least not in the eyes of a search engine. To market your webinar effectively through a press release, you must know how search engines work. Below are some tips to help your press release rise to the top of the list when some company executive or manager surfs the web to keep up with the newest thing in the field.

Use keywords in the title. Remember no one will be using the word webinar in a news engine search. And if your company is well known, people may be looking for news on that as well. Use something like "Spud Corp. Offers Webinar for Hazardous Waste Engineers Handling Toxic Organic Compounds."

Mention keywords in the first paragraph. The first paragraph is where search engine rubber meets the road. It's where people decide what the press release is all about. Whatever you do, don't use any keyword more than two times, because the search engine then begins to think this is commercial spam and not a real news item.

Put a worded hotlink to your site in the first paragraph. Most business news readers scan only the first paragraph, so don't put the contact link at the bottom of the page. Write the press release first and then go back and find the right place to put your website link that way the link doesn't look like "marketing" but just part of the release.

Use proper anchor text. Search engines actually read the words in your link not only to determine how to rank your press release, but also to see if your landing page (which should be the webinar registration page) should be listed on the search engine.

--To Charge or Not To Charge – and How Much?

With any kind of event or class, virtual or real, no matter how much interest people have in it, if you don't charge money, people stay away in droves. Seems counterintuitive, but almost any kind of event where tickets or reservations are given out free-of-charge will have high no-show rates— on the order of 35 percent or more. In comparison, when people have to pay real money, even if it's a relatively modest amount, no-show rates drop to 5 percent or less.

People understand that "you get what you pay for," especially in business or any kind of competitive arena. Marketers commonly mistakenly think that the cheaper you make something, the more people will be able to afford it and therefore want to buy it. When you're talking about information transfer, however, this just does not apply. Instead, your price tag tells people what you think your information is worth. Make sure that what you charge matches the importance of the information you're providing and/or the credentials of the person presenting the information.

In terms of the latter, remember that you would not expect to pay $5 to hear management tips from General Colin Powell. If you saw that advertised, you'd think it was a scam. Some people would pay hundreds of dollars just to hear him speak, even if the topic were something of only peripheral interest, just to hear his perspective. So keep the credentials of your presenter in mind when setting your price.

--Nonverbals Are Still Important, Even on a Webinar

When you're speaking in public, audiences are influenced by your body language even more than they are by the words you're saying. In well-known study, Albert Mehrabian, a professor at UCLA, developed the 7%-38%-55% Rule.[1] The percentages reflect what part of total communication is conveyed by words (7%), tone of voice (38%), and body language (55%).

Taking away one of these parts ups the ante on your brain's reaction to another. If you're on a teleconference, where people can't see you, suddenly the words become that much more important. But in a videoconference, you're suddenly at the mercy of all these things.

Nerves can be read easily when you're in front of a crowd, and being able to move can sometimes hide the little shakes until you gain your footing and feel more confident. Most of the time on a videoconference you're glued to one place, however, so it's difficult to walk off the nervous feelings and find ways to make your fears less apparent. What can be done to prepare for a webinar in which you'll be the center of attention?

Even if your webinar won't include videoconferencing, it will almost certainly include some sort of speaking. So your first goal should be to make sure your voice is clear and concise. Sure, it's only 7 percent of the total communication, but if participants can't see you, then what you're saying becomes so much more important. And the key to effective words is research. In many ways, the business world is like college, where you could probably skip a few nights in the library and still get a passing grade, but no professor will nominate your presentation for an award.

Now, if you had spent a few extra hours in the library, your presentation could have probably been more effective.

In the business world, you should treat every presentation as if it's the audience's first time hearing the information. Give the basics, offer a place where they can get more information, and then dig into the meat of the topic. Not only does it make your audience feel more at home, but it also gives you a jumping-off point where you feel more comfortable before getting into less-familiar territory.

When it comes to a videoconference, be aware of your body language and posture.[2] You'll usually be sitting down; sit up straight and look directly into the camera. Since eye contact is most important for connecting with your audience, and since they're not right in front of you, imagine that staring into the camera is the same as looking at your participants.

Leaning forward when listening to another's comments or being asked a question not only indicates a readiness to act, but also an interest in what the other person is saying. Tilting your head also expresses interest in the things being said and done around you. Nodding while another person is speaking indicates an understanding of what's being asked or said.

Above all, you need to remember that people can see your face. So if you roll your eyes or make uncomfortable facial expressions, it will be apparent that you're questioning the information being presented.

In the end, being comfortable with the information you're giving will be the greatest influence over audience perception. When you know what you're talking about the information will come easily, and any nerves you may have will soon dissipate. Confidence is the key. Do your research, know your subject, know your audience, and things will be much easier.[3] Develop the presentation, design the slides, and display your incredible skills.

1 http://en.wikipedia.org/wiki/Albert_Mehrabian

2 http://www.coping.org/dialogue/nonverbal.htm#What

3 http://www.accuconference.com/blog/5StepsToAGreat Presentation.aspx

Part Four: The Visual Presentation

-- Designing Top-Notch Slide Presentations

The broader focus of constructing slide presentations entails figuring out which piece of your presentation goes on which slide and how to connect them all into a cohesive whole. Here's a proven approach:

Translate your presentation structure into draft slides. You'll need an opening slide (usually an inspiring image or quote) and an agenda slide (a table of contents for your presentation; this is different from the quick synopsis of your key points, which is part of your presentation). Then you'll need slides for all your main points and backup slides (at least one or two) to support those main points. And finally, you'll need a closing (or summary) slide. So how many slides in total does that give you? Use one piece of paper for each (or, if you're already using your slide software program, map out the number you'll need there).

Connect the agenda and the main points and backup slides. Use the same wording throughout. For instance, if you describe the employee handbook as the "Employee Guide," use that throughout your presentation so as not to confuse anyone. Keep the typography and graphics, spacing, amount of text, and size of text as similar as you can through all the slides. Another idea is to repeat that agenda slide throughout the presentation, each time you switch to the next main point. But do that only if your presentation is complicated and really requires people to focus on how each main point relates to the others.

Choose colors that don't overwhelm or distract from your text. If you use PowerPoint, avoid the templates that come with the program, suggests PowerPoint critic Edward Tufte, who said, "No matter how beautiful your PP readymade template is, it would be better if there were less of it." Design your own template and then keep it consistent, as mentioned in step 2. Use a solid background, without patterns or textures or graphics that move. Avoid bright colors and neons. Be aware of the font colors you place on top of the background color. If you select a darker background, the font color needs to be lighter, and the same is true for the opposite.

Keep the typography simple, and ignore the urge to add animated or convoluted graphics. Less is much more; trust me. I recently took a multimedia presentation class and realized that every presentation I've ever given was a disgrace to the name presentation. I love animation and graphics and pretty colors. By the time I got out of that class, I knew I would never again subject my audience to a dancing cartoon character or a headline that flickers on the screen. Resist the thought that a fancy graphic or animation will add pizzazz to your boring presentation. Above all, remember that the slide show should accompany a solid presentation. Use your abilities as a public speaker to mix with your presentation to get the most positive response from your audience. Tell stories about what you've learned along the way, how you've learned these lessons, and the participants will hang on to your every word and slide.

-- Creating Effective PowerPoint Slides

The second stage of designing your presentation is to build the individual slides to best convey your overall message. Here are the key principles:

Each slide needs a title. It's confusing to come into the middle of a presentation, having missed the first five minutes, and see a slide without any identifying information. It's a graph, with lots of numbers, but the late-arriving attendee has no idea what the numbers represent and has to dig through his handout or ask someone for information. Why not just put a headline on it? It's an easy, straightforward, audience-friendly approach.

Titles are not all equal. Communications specialist Mary Munter calls good titles "message titles" and bad titles "topic titles." A topic title is something like "Our Company," while a message title is "Our Company's Growth in 2008." Many presentation templates emphasize the use of topic titles (for those presenters throwing together their slides at the last minute), but take a few more minutes and think it through. How can you best explain what's on that slide? What message do you want to send?

Use graphs, word charts, and concept diagrams. Slide after slide of text is not the best approach. If your information can be presented another way, why not try it? Most presentation programs provide a variety of chart options. If you're presenting several "how much" or "how" concepts, consider doing so with charts, graphs, or concept diagrams. Rather than just using a bulleted list, why not use a visual representation? Some of the options in a program like PowerPoint are over the top and unnecessary, but a simple chart here and there can spice up an otherwise unfriendly presentation.

It depends on their learning style. Graphs and charts will help the half of your audience who are visual learners, and they'll also hold the interest of the other half who are verbal or aural learners.

-- The Power of Presentation Visuals

Here's a question to ask yourself: Do people retain information by reading it or by understanding connections between it and other information? Whether in a live speech or a web conference, the content of your presentations can be greatly enhanced by visuals. The audience can't see you in the latter case, but you can still put documents, graphs, and video in front of their eyes with perfect timing. If your visuals are subpar, however, will your presentation be greatly affected? According to Dave Paradi, poor visuals can only lessen, not destroy, the impact of a presentation.[1]

Paradi's example was of a lecture by an esteemed academic and expert in his field. While his studies and conclusions were well-researched and presented clearly, the visuals were poor and not used effectively. But Paradi says the presentation was well received anyway. His conclusion is that "great content will trump poor visuals." Audience members will leave informed and enlightened, but not to the extent they could have been.

I agree with Paradi regarding live speeches. When you stand in front of an audience, you are the presentation, not your visuals. Your words and body language can only be enhanced by pictures, video, and such. For a web conference presentation, however, I disagree completely; great content can be sunk by poor visuals. After all, in a web conference only your voice and visuals drive the presentation. If the graphs are confusing, the pictures blurry, and the documents not spell-checked, the participants can be greatly distracted from what you're saying.

However, I do like Paradi's solution, and it's even more effective for web conferences: Create the presentation and the visuals separately. Don't fire up PowerPoint and use it to create your outline and main points. Don't look for pictures to talk about. Leave all but a blank page to write your presentation, and only afterward find great visuals to enhance the content of your speech.

1   http://pptideas.blogspot.com/2008/11/does-great-content-trump-poor-visuals.html

-- Do's and Don'ts of Using Color on Presentation Slides

When it comes to creating our slide presentations, concerns are usually focused on making the slides entertaining and informative. When we start putting our slides together, we start to think of ways that we can achieve our desired results. We have all been guilty of breaking the rules and over animating or putting far too many graphics on our slides. The temptation is there to make your slides bright and colorful, but you could be doing more harm than good.

The first thing you have to know when it comes to coloring your slide presentations is to know what colors are complimentary. Just like in fashion, you want your slides to be appealing to the eyes of your audience and you don't want your colors to clash. If you wouldn't wear bright yellow pants and a lime green shirt (which, please do not do this – ever) why would you want to make people look at it on a slideshow? Use a color wheel if you want to double check yourself to make sure that your colors complement each other. On a color wheel, complimentary colors are across from each other.

Once you know what colors complement each other, you can start adding them into your presentations. Remember to use dark text with light backgrounds or vice versa. Trying to stick yellow text on pink backgrounds will only give your audience a headache. Your goal with a slide show is to make them look at your slides. The last thing you want is for them to go running from the room screaming, "My eyes are bleeding!"

Extra Tip: Pick one combination of colors and stick with it throughout the whole presentation.

There is an entire psychology about color and how the colors that we see can evoke certain emotions in our brains. Red is associated with energy and power, whereas yellow is associated with joy and happiness. Knowing how the colors might affect your audience will help you know which colors might be the best combinations to use.

You can spice up your presentations in a number of ways, but be careful when you start throwing colors and graphics into your slides. Slides should make your audience pay attention, not make them think that you are completely nuts. How are you using color in your slide presentations? Are you playing it safe with all black and white? If you are using color, how do you decide what colors to use?

-- PowerPoint Tips for the "Presentationally Impaired"

Bad presenters are like tone-deaf singers: they don't know how bad they really are. Whatever your skill level, here are some tips that will point you in the right direction, no matter if you're getting started or just looking for some ways to update your current style of presentations:

The 10/20/30 Rule. This tip, from Guy Kawasaki, stands for 10 slides, 20 minutes, and 30-point font.[1] Use this formula as you develop and revise your next Power-Point. Remember that the average person can only comprehend about 10 different concepts in one sitting. Keep your presentation under 20 minutes to ensure that you leave enough time for Q & A and that you don't bore listeners with too much information. Lastly, using a 30-point font will force you to use fewer words and make your slides easier to understand.

Six Words Per Slide. So why use fewer words? Seth Godin, best-selling author and marketing consultant, suggests no more than six words on a slide, ever. He says that PowerPoint is meant to complement you as the speaker and not become a replacement. He suggests using captivating images and catchy headers that will blend well with what you're saying. The fewer the words and the better the image, the more memorable the slide will be.[2]

Cue Cards and Handouts. If you limit the number of words for each slide, you should make yourself cue cards to remember the details. You should also create a handout with important information for your audience. But don't provide the handout until after the presentation or people might leave early or become distracted by your notes. (For a contrary view on when to distribute handouts, see "Handout Tips" later in this book.)

1 http://blog.guykawasaki.com/2005/12/the_102030_rule.html

2 http://sethgodin.typepad.com/seths_blog/2007/01/really_bad_powe.html

-- Freeing Yourself from the PowerPoint Security Blanket

When you think meetings, do you think PowerPoint slides? I sure do. Every meeting I'm in these days (offline and online) is always the same: the same slides and the speaker who, somewhere along the way, forgets how good he or she is and just starts to read the slides. Yawn. Here are a few tips to get out from under your PowerPoint security blanket:

Tell stories with your slides. A story is a 100% improvement over the usual charts and graphs slideshow. When talking about how to sell ice cream, use ice cream as the visual. If you are telling a story about your dog, show the audience a picture of him. If you are talking about something that happened to you on vacation, put up a picture of the beach you were on. Stories create a scene in the audience's mind, and pictures help them to see the scene better.

Try to consider whether you even need slides for your speech. A nicely designed slide show can really show you off, but a slide for every single thing you say can quickly overpower your presence and become the focal point of your presentation. Can you just skip it during your next speech? Wouldn't it be nice not to have to compete with a machine for your audience's attention?

A slide of vapid statistics really has no meaning. If you want to report those statistics, why not put them into context? You don't want to make people use their calculators to understand your presentation. Present the crucial numbers in a way that can be easily understood. "This year we'll see a 67 percent growth in our international division." That's an easy thing for attendees to jot down.

After you've designed your PowerPoint presentation, print out a copy of the slides, but only to make brief notes.

Many speakers used this printed copy of slides to note at what point they wish to change the slides. If you want to be sure to change the slide when you start to present the topic of bunny rabbits, you can note that on the printed page. Never write your entire speech on this paper – this should be used as a guide only.

Remember Seth Godin's rule of thumb: no more than six words on a slide. If you think Seth's advice is crazy, check out his astute guide to PowerPoint.[1] If you're still not convinced, think back to the best presentation you ever sat through, and try to copy your next presentation to match. I'll bet it was succinct and sparse, right?

Follow even one of these rules and you'll be giving better presentations than most corporations in America. Don't your employees and clients deserve that from you?

1 http://www.sethgodin.typepad.com/seths_blog/2007/01/really_bad_powe.html

-- Reading from PowerPoint Slides – You Should Know Better

I recently attended a conference and noticed something that was very disturbing that seemed to be going around among the speakers. It wasn't the Black Death, nor was it some unspeakable disease that was going to ravish us all. It was much worse. There were a lot of well-respected speakers who were reading directly from their presentation slides.

The temptation to do so is always there but if you find yourself taking this path, you can do some quick things to break up the monotony.

Ad Lib. Don't be afraid to throw in a story off the cuff. It's okay to mention things you didn't have written down in your notes; you just don't want to travel off too far on a tangent.

Give More Visual Cues. Instead of trying to cram a lot of text on your slides, use carefully chosen graphics to let your audience know what's in store, and use the graphics as a place holder for your presentation. This way you'll know where you are in the speech.

Invite Participants to Give Feedback. This is a great idea, especially if it is your first time making a presentation in front of a crowd. Your participants can really help you figure out where you did great and where you could use improvement. Don't be afraid to ask.

There is a level of concern that crops up when we realize that we must do two things at once, like speaking and advancing slides. Our minds convince us that the best thing to do is to use the presentation slides as our guide for our speech, but it only causes us to rely on them more than we should. It won't help you overcome any of your nerves or anxiety.

--Ten Ways Webinars Can Boost Your Business, Starting Today

Chris Garrett is an Internet marketing consultant and business blogger living in the UK. Chris was kind enough to write this for the AccuConference blog a few years ago and we wanted to make sure that it was included in our book.

Business can benefit from teleseminars and webinars much more than merely holding your standard conference call. Due to my lack of vocal confidence, I resisted doing much of this kind of thing for a while, until I finally took the plunge. Now I regret holding off as long as I did, because my income and audience have vastly improved each time I've tried one of the kinds of teleseminar or webinar I list below. Check them out and see how they could fit into your business.

1. List-Building Webinar. The first positive impact you can see from holding a webinar is email list opt-ins. This could be all the reason you need for putting one on. Even better, these are good leads, people who really want to hear from you. They have taken action and cleared their schedules for an hour, making them much better prospects than people who are only kinda-sorta interested in what you have to say.

2. Brainstorms. They say two heads are better than one, but what about five or ten? I know many folks who have regular, formal brainstorms and get great value from them. I, on the other hand, have a few people I get together with on an ad hoc basis, but I still find the experience indispensable.

3. Regular Call/Radio Show/Podcast. Sometimes all it takes is for your customers to get to know your voice in order for them to warm to you. This can be achieved by running a regular call, radio show, or podcast. Put it in a specific and regular time slot so people can tune in each time, and that will grow familiarity, personal connection, and trust.

4. One-Off Buzz-Building Event. Rather than a regu-

lar show, what about a one-off? Events are a perfect way to build word-of-mouth buzz and anticipation. You can use the event for publicity, to generate links, to build traffic, and to gain attention for a message or product launch.

5. Authority-Building Interview Series. Borrow credibility, expertise, and authority from thought leaders in your market. Interview them and get vital nuggets of wisdom to share with your prospects and customers.

6. Paid Membership Club. If you have access to lots of experts with great information, turn it into a revenue opportunity by charging for access and sharing the proceeds with your interviewees.

7. Online Audio Course. Put your own expertise into a curriculum and sell it. You might think this will eat into your product sales or consulting service or divert attention from your core business, but everyone I've spoken to who has done this has found the reverse to be true. More people buy their consulting and products, more readily, because they know the company is the right one to help with their problem.

8. Q&A. Instead of answering the same questions over and over in email or one-to-one, put together a question-and-answer call. This will overcome sales objections, help customers with tricky challenges, and demonstrate your commitment to customer service.

9. Product Preview/Overview/Demonstration. Sometimes customers don't know what they don't know. Demonstrating a product can both educate in the

use of the product and explain the benefits, and it serves as "proof" when the prospects can see the before and after with their own eyes. It doesn't have to be live or even video; a logical sequence of slides, explained well, can work just as effectively.

10. Digital Product. Finally, when you have all these calls or webinars recorded, why not add a transcript and sell or give away the recording and booklet? You might use them as freebies or offer them for sale at a profit. This can be a quick and easy way to create information products.

In summary, think beyond conference calls and look at all the other ways you can benefit from webinars and telephone seminars.

You can find Chris Garrett at his own blog http://chrisg.com

www.ingramcontent.com/pod-product-compliance
Lightning Source LLC
Chambersburg PA
CBHW051539170526
45165CB00002B/792